MY REASON FOR HOPE

MY REASON FOR HOPE

Andrew Swift

Authentic

MILTON KEYNES ● COLORADO SPRINGS ● HYDERABAD

First published 2008 by Authentic Media
9 Holdom Avenue, Bletchley, Milton Keynes, MK1 1QR, UK
1820 Jet Stream Drive, Colorado Springs, CO 80921, USA
OM Authentic Media, Medchal Road, Jeedimetla Village,
Secunderabad 500 055, A.P., India
www.authenticmedia.co.uk

Authentic Media is a division of IBS-STL U.K., limited by guarantee, with its
Registered Office at Kingstown Broadway, Carlisle, Cumbria CA3 0HA.
Registered in England & Wales No. 1216232. Registered charity 270162

British Library Cataloguing in Publication Data
A catalogue record for this book is available from the British Library
ISBN-13: 978-1-85078-790-7

Cover Design by fourninezero design.
Print Management by Adare
Printed in Great Britain by J.H. Haynes & Co., Sparkford

Contents

To all 'prisoners of hope'
Zechariah 9:12

. . . finding a fresh sense of God's hope in your life . . .

With thanks to . . .

My beautiful wife Vicki for her support
Andy Frost for his unwavering encouragement and the use of his contacts,
All those who contributed their 'reason for hope',
My parents who enabled me to build the firm foundations in my life,
Special thanks to my proof readers Jan Vickers, Mary Bunker and John Swift, and the fantastic Authentic Media Team, Charlotte Hubback and Kath Williams.
And most of all . . . to God who is my firm foundation.

Foreword

These appear to be dark days; gun crime; global poverty; the war on terror; the AIDS epidemic; drug abuse; human trafficking. Stories of hopelessness drip feed into our souls and begin to take root. They overwhelm us with a sense of despair and it's often easy to lose all hope.

But there is a hope and Andi's book is a desperate call to rediscover this vital truth.

My Reason for Hope is a timely resource that reminds us of the hope that we have . . . a hope that cannot be defeated . . . a hope that cannot be overcome . . . a hope that will stand the test of time.

This hope is more than a human hope. It is more than a 'hope' for good weather or a 'hope' for the train to be on time. This is a hope that is found in Jesus – an eternal promise of what will be. This hope is not fantasy.

Hope is sparked when something of eternity bursts into our fragile lives. For a moment we lift our eyes from the problems of the world and glimpse things as they could be, as they will be.

When Andi first came to me with the concept for this book, I knew that this message of hope was important but I was sceptical about the whole idea. My fear was that we would have a set of similar stories that repeated themselves. But as I began to read, I discovered that they are all so different. Each story carries its own perspective, its own viewpoint.

The contributors come from contrasting spheres of life. Each writer has met with God and been profoundly impacted. There is no bland uniform response but a beautiful tapestry of stories that point to eternity.

As we read these stories, we begin to share in their hope and something mystical happens: change within ourselves. These people have discovered hope and are taking seriously the commission to be carriers of hope to a broken world. Hope invading despair.

This book is inspiration for these seemingly dark days. Though we live in the shadow of despair, we know that the clouds will clear and that hope will reign.

Thank you, Andi, for writing this book and allowing me to rediscover a fresh sense of God's hope in my life. Thank you for taking that risk to follow through with what God has inspired.

I hope, as you read this collection, you, like me, will discover a fresh sense of hope as God speaks to your heart.

Andy Frost

Introduction: Hope

Hope. A word that conjures up deep emotions in us all: hope for our family, hope for our crime-ridden cities, hope for our nation, hope for a dying world, hope for wealth, hope for our health and hope for an afterlife.

This book is a collection of brief stories of how a variety of people from diverse backgrounds put their hope in God. You will read of how they have come through a journey of discovery and realized that true hope can only be found in him.

I trust that as you read these stories you will be inspired to question your own hope. Some of you have been Christians since childhood, some may have come to Christ more recently, but we are all called to prepare ourselves to account for our own hope: 'Always be prepared to give an answer to everyone who asks you to give the reason for the hope that you have' (1 Pet. 3:15).

I don't believe our accounts are solely for non-Christians to hear: they are also essential for our own ears. As we speak our reason for hope, we are doing something in the spiritual realm: our spoken words of hope will minister to our own hearts. The words of hope of others will strengthen our faith and confidence in God.

What is hope?

A general view is that hope is a belief in a positive outcome. The Collins English Dictionary states that hope is 'to desire, usually with some possibility of fulfilment'. It implies a certain amount of perseverance, steadfastness and uncertainty. It is an emotion that all humans experience. But hope for a Christian expresses more than a mere longing, or a vague possibility that everything will turn out all right in the end. We believe that a positive outcome is absolutely certain even when there is evidence to the contrary.

The word 'hope' is used over one hundred and thirty times in the Bible. In the New Testament the Greek word predominantly used is *ëlpis*. The primary origin of this word is *ëlpõ*, which means 'to anticipate, usually with pleasure, expectation and confidence'. I love this definition. We have a hope that not only brings us confidence, but pleasure.

The writer of Hebrews puts it this way, 'faith is being sure of what we hope for, and certain of what we do not see' (11:1). In other words, what we have hope in is revealed by our actions and what we say: the tangible substance of life. Hebrews continues to describe some incredible actions which people did by faith because they had absolute hope in God's promises.

One example is Moses. Most people know how Moses escaped Pharaoh, came out of Egypt, crossed the Red Sea and then wandered around the wilderness for forty years. Whilst everyone was moaning and groaning, Moses kept the vision of hope that God had showed to him: the Promised Land. The Israelites quickly forgot God's promise and how he had saved them from Pharaoh and destroyed the Egyptian army, but for forty years Moses kept the hope deep within himself.

David is another excellent example. At the beginning of Psalm 43 David outlines his sense of utter hopelessness. Nevertheless, in the following verses he voices the hope that he has in God. He cries aloud to God to send his light into his dark circumstances.

David often speaks to his own soul, declaring hope into himself. The world often says we should accept our feelings, that we can't help how we feel. It says we can't help whom we fall in love with and that we must accept how our heart reacts. But the Bible teaches us that we need to say truth to our soul. We are not governed by our own feelings. We need to speak to bitterness; we need to speak to downcast souls that our hope is in Jesus. We must grow in this hope which we have and share it with others.

At times people may question why we need to speak words of faith and hope out loud. Often preachers, during a service, ask their congregation to repeat key phrases or quotes from the Bible. It might sound an odd request, but in my experience speaking out words of faith and hope does something positive in your spirit. Your expectation of the fulfilment of God's promises will increase as you do so.

As you read the testimonies, you will see how most people initially put their hope in worldly things, only to find that these do not bring fulfilment. They eventually come to find that their ultimate hope is found in Jesus Christ. The basis of this is in the promises and prophecies of God. Once this hope is found, these people have taken personal responsibility to build a relationship with the hope provider – God – and to share their newfound hope with others. As it says in Colossians 1:27, 'Christ in you, the hope of glory'.

Hope – the eternal perspective

We get to live on this earth on average for almost eighty years, but we will spend eternity somewhere else. I believe that if we confess with our mouths and believe in our heart that Jesus rose from the dead, and we invite him into our lives, then we will spend and enjoy eternity in heaven.

Having a living hope and a hope in God's glory should affect our lives now. My dad, when seeing the way I drive, compares me to being a Formula One driver. He always says I need to have an eternal perspective when driving: take my time; let others in; bless them; and follow Jesus' instructions on living a godly life.

Smith Wigglesworth refers to this living hope and eternal perspective.

> If Christ rose not, our faith is in vain, we are yet in our sins, it has no foundation. But Christ has risen and become the first fruits, and we have now the glorious hope that we shall be so changed. We who were not a people are now the people of God. Born out of the due time, out of the mire, to be among princes. Beloved, God wants us to see the preciousness of it. It will drive away the dullness of life; it is here set above all other things. Jesus gave all for this treasure. He purchased the field because of the pearl, the pearl of great price – the substratum of humanity. Jesus purchased it, and we are the pearl of great price for all time. Our inheritance is in Heaven.

Let us inspire each other in the hope we have found, and our future glory with God.

The hope of Jesus Christ is available to everyone. It is available to all those who hunger and thirst. This hope is for the poor in spirit, those who are broken-hearted and those who appear to be living a comfortable life. I make a promise that when you find this hope it will not be washed away like sand. It's a hope that will wonderfully change your life now and bring fullness and joy.

Let's share our hope with everyone.

Bibliography

Liardon, R., *Smith Wigglesworth: The Complete Collection of His Life Teachings* (Tulsa, Oklahoma: Albury Publishing, 1996)

HarperCollins, *The Collins Paperback English Dictionary* (London: HarperColllins, 1999)

Strong, J., *The New Strong's Exhaustive Concordance of the Bible* (Nashville, Tennessee: Thomas Nelson Publishers, 1996)

One

Church Leaders

One

Church Leaders

Gerald Coates

Gerald Coates is best known as a Christian communicator and regularly appears in magazines and newspapers, on the radio and TV. He founded the Pioneer Trust, which works with those in and beyond the church, offering help, advice, provision and care. He has written nine books, including Non-Religious Christianity.

I am not merely an optimist – I am completely captivated by hope.

I believe for the best – when I prepare for the worst.

I'm sixty-three years of age. I've been married to my wife Anona for forty years and I have three grown-up sons, and between us we pray for hope in the darkest situations. And as a parent, you face all the challenges of children growing up, doing silly and dangerous things or adopting attitudes that are harmful to themselves or others.

But 'love never gives up', as one writer put it.

It is difficult not to 'give up' if you have no hope. Once you've lost hope you can get careless, sloppy and turn to all sorts of damaging things.

Ever since I was young, I knew the basic story of humanity gone wrong, damaging ourselves and one another at a personal, local, national and international level. Despite our own privileges and pleasures, overall the world is not a happy place.

Some put their hope in money. A rich man died and someone asked 'How much did he leave?' The answer?

'Everything'. Nothing lasts forever. Some put their hope in people, but they often fail.

Is there something or someone we can put our hope into? Who will pull us through the darkness and provide the silver lining to the clouds of life?

I have found that person to be Jesus Christ.

The unique thing about Christianity is that its founder saw the world go wrong and do wrong, and unintentionally and sometimes intentionally, damage one another. So he became one of us. A baby, a boy, a teenager, a young man, and then took the penalty for all the wrongdoing we have done, at a cross on Calvary.

In a moral universe God cannot wink at wrongdoing, murder, rape, stealing and lying and pretend it doesn't matter. It does – to you and to me. Do you think it would be right for unrepentant killers of children, rapists, torturers and dictators who lead their country into turmoil to be in heaven?

So as a teenager I put my trust and hope in Christ. Not only for forgiveness, cleansing and receiving a new Spirit (the Holy Spirit), but I put my hope in him for life, death and beyond.

Like you, the reader, I have been let down by others, betrayed, lied about and had rumours whispered in ears and posted on the internet. But I've had the privilege of influencing millions of lives through public speaking, writing songs and appearing in the media.

There's hope in me and millions upon millions of Christians around the world because he not only lived and died but raised himself from the dead. And he lives today. He's living in ordinary mothers and fathers, sons and daughters, among our youth workers, social workers, teachers, doctors, nurses and MPs and many more – whose lives have been changed because they've found a reason for hope in Jesus Christ. Hope for a better world and another world.

Chat show host Michael Parkinson was interviewing the Chief Rabbi who was known to be both profound and humorous. Parkinson asked, 'Where was God in the holocaust?' and reminded him of the loss of family, boyhood friends, colleagues and academics.

The Rabbi answered 'God was there.'

Parkinson became confused, his brow furrowing, and asked 'How could God be there? This wasn't heaven on earth, it was hell.'

The Rabbi paused. 'God was there and I can tell you, he was saying, "Thou shalt not kill." But nobody was listening.'

I hope (there's that word again) that you are listening as you read these stories of women and men whose lives were changed because of the hope that Jesus Christ puts in someone.

Compared to the Creator of the universe and the hero Jesus Christ, who gave such brilliant and profound perspectives and teachings on life, we may at times feel we are worthless. But the death of Jesus revalues us all. The offer of a new start and fresh hope is there for you and your friends today.

Will Van Der Hart

Reverend Will Van Der Hart is Associate Vicar at St Mary's Bryanston Square, London, and Director of Mind and Soul, a website which explores the links between Christianity and mental health. He is a passionate evangelist and works across the city with students and young professionals. Will is married to Lucinda, a journalist.

Have you ever tried to show someone a shooting star? Staring up at the vast expanse of sky for a millisecond's worth of streaking silver light? You wait and wait and then shout, 'Look, there!' with increasing exasperation. Hope does not often come through prescription but through standing with another. Hope is brought not by seeing the star but through standing next to one who sees it. Like two fishermen on a pond, when one man's float darts under, the other is challenged out of his despondency; he is awakened to believe that soon his float too will dart under the glassy surface.

We are all born with a level of hope in the tank: a bit like the new car that we drive off the showroom forecourt. It gets you a little way, enough to realize you could go further. If only you put a little more fuel in, you could travel, you could see things you had never seen, experience what could be experienced, maybe even end up at the destination you had imagined in your mind's eye.

The thing about this 'born with' hope is that if it isn't really renewed, what happens then? This generation is often uncomfortable, limping, awkward. I can't help but think that it is a generation that has not been refilled; somehow it has lost hope, like a band of shell-shocked soldiers, there is a vacancy in their eyes. But maybe, to some anyway, to lose something is to find something. They say, 'You don't know what you had until it's gone.' You certainly know when hope is gone, its unwelcome relative, despair, moves in to the space left.

It seems odd to be saying that my reason for hope is having none. That's not what I mean. You see, there is always hope. I work with the broken, the damaged, the abused, the restless. I stand with people who claim to have no hope. My job is to show them some. I am a priest and a priest, they say, 'stands in the gap'. Of course I don't believe that; I am no more in front of them than I am behind them, I am with them, not other than them.

I am an ex-hopeless. I have seen Jesus and I stand next to many who have not. Yet my reason for hope is that through my seeing, they soon will also see. There is in my experience and my understanding, nothing on earth, nothing known or unknown to us that can bring hope like this man. He is in himself both fully God and fully human. In so being he did stand in the gap, dying and rising in my place. Jesus is the locus for all my hopes and I have the compass in my pocket. I navigate hope like the seamen of old, by the Son.

Brian Broderson

Brian Broderson has been involved in pastoral ministry for over twenty years. He served as Senior Pastor of Calvary Chapel Vista, California, and as Senior Pastor of Calvary Chapel Westminster. Brian has also been extensively involved in missionary work throughout Europe. He is now Associate Pastor at Calvary Chapel Costa Mesa and is the featured speaker on the Bible teaching program Back to Basics. *Brian and his wife Cheryl have four children and two grandchildren.*

Hope is one of those things that I didn't have much of as a kid growing up in the suburbs of Los Angeles. My parents broke up when I was around five years old and I was the only boy with three younger sisters. A few years later my mom remarried. That was the beginning of a long road of frustration, trying to adjust to a stepfather with whom I had absolutely nothing in common. Looking back, those seemed like pretty hopeless times. When I reached my early teens, I fell in love with surfing. Finally I had found something that I loved doing. It wasn't too long before I was fairly good at it, at least good enough to get some local recognition. Surfing now has become a popular sport, but back in the late 1960s surfing was more a way of life, a sub-culture where you connected with other surfers, the sea and nature itself. A big part of connecting with nature was enjoying the herbs that nature provided, particularly cannabis. So at the ripe old age of thirteen, I began to smoke dope and eventually experiment with many other, not so natural, chemicals. For almost the next ten years I lived in the world of surf, sex, drugs and rock-n-roll. Those of my mindset thought, we were 'the people'. We looked hip, we looked cool, and we looked like trendsetters having the time of our lives.

Reality was a bit different. We were frustrated, empty, lonely, angry and above all hopeless. At least this was my experience. I would later find that this was also the case with many of my friends as well. However, at the time, no one dared to let the 'cat out of the bag'.

The longer I travelled that road the more depressing it got. Not only was I well accepted in the surf crowd, I was also the lead singer for one of the hottest bands in town. As a matter of fact, our first gig was to open for a well-known artist whose hit song was 'Hot Child in the City'. We appeared to be on the fast track to rock stardom. With Hollywood just up the road, we could see ourselves playing the Roxie or the Whiskey in no time at all. With all of the excitement of that first gig I was completely shocked when the night ended and I was left standing there alone feeling the emptiest I'd ever had. What went wrong? Why had such a sense of futility seized my mind? I needed to find out.

I had never really been religious. However, I did have an admiration for Jesus Christ and some kind of belief that he might have something to do with my life. So, frustrated and hopeless, I decided to pick up the family Bible and see what it had to say. When I read through the Gospel of Matthew I was absolutely astounded. I felt that this man Jesus was speaking directly to me. These are the words I remember reading,

> "Come to me, all you who are weary and burdened, and I will give you rest. Take my yoke upon you and learn from me, for I am gentle and humble in heart, and you

will find rest for your souls. For my yoke is easy and my burden is light." (11:28–29)

'Rest for your soul . . . ': that's what I had been searching for but didn't know it until that moment. A short while later I surrendered my life to the living Jesus Christ.

The emptiness, the frustration, the hopelessness vanished that day to never return. I have peace and hope. My hope is in Christ, in his plan for my life, and in his promise to give me a place in his kingdom for all eternity. I hope you'll receive that hope by reaching out to the One who loves you and died in your place to prove it.

God bless.

Rob Frost

Andy Frost writes: Just before this book was finished, Rob was promoted to glory. In the midst of mourning the loss of a great mentor, boss and most importantly, Dad, it has been great to read these words of 'hope'. He wrote these words just a short time before his death. As a follower of Jesus, Rob knew his final destination and that was to be with his Heavenly Father.

Rob Frost was in great demand as a preacher. He was an International Director of the International Leadership Institute based in Atlanta. He authored twenty-five books, and presented Premier Radio's flagship current affairs programme 'Frost On Sunday'. Rob Frost lectured at London School of Theology, was President Emeritus of Share Jesus International, an ecumenical mission agency, and was President of Release International.

Over the last few weeks I've spent a lot of time hanging around cancer clinics. Not something I had planned for, nor expected. Some of them are stark, bare places where a picture on the wall or a vase of flowers would have made such a difference. Sometimes, even a chair to sit on would have been a bonus. It's focused my mind. Where is my ultimate hope? In the doctors, in myself, in the latest therapies or treatments? Or, in fact, do I have a greater hope than all of these?

A friend of mine once attended a wrestling match in which a 'caped crusader' was fighting a rather weak-looking figure who seemed destined to lose from the very start. As the match continued the caped crusader became more and more aggressive, throwing his opponent around the ring with complete abandon.

The fight got more and more out of control, until the caped crusader flung his opponent out of the ring, and when the referee protested, he threw him out of the ring, too! Just then, as the so called 'victor' pranced about the ring proclaiming himself the champion, the spotlight slowly swung round to the entrance to the hall.

There, standing in the doorway, was the famous wrestler Big Daddy. Slowly and confidently he strode down the aisle, hauled himself into the ring and threw the self-proclaimed 'champion' out of the ring. He leant over the ropes and pulled the referee and the 'weaker' wrestler back into the ring. He reached out his hands and lifted the arms of the 'defeated' wrestler high. He who had seemingly been defeated was now the winner.

My friend told me that here, in a wrestling ring, he saw a parable of the defeat of Satan and, the ultimate victory of one whom the crowd thought was powerless and defeated.

This is the paradox of the cross. Just when Jesus looked as though he was humiliated and defeated, his Father was beginning to usher in the greatest victory of all.

When I face real challenges in my work, family or health – and it seems as though the devil has got the 'upper hand' – I reach for my Bible and read about the 'New Jerusalem' in Revelation 21 and remember that there is a new time coming.

> I heard a voice thunder from the Throne: "Look! Look! God has moved into the neighbourhood, making his home with men and women! They're his people, He's their God. He'll wipe away every tear from their eyes.

Death is gone for good—tears gone, crying gone, pain gone—all the first order of things gone." (Rev. 21:3–5, The Message)

Mark Pease

Mark Pease and his wife, Hannah, are pastors of El-Shaddai International Christian Centre, Cardiff. Mark is passionately committed to seeing communities restored in every way: spiritually, socially, emotionally, physically and financially. His other passions in life are music, sport and his two daughters.

My name is Mark and I am thirty-four years old. I'm married and have two beautiful daughters. I'm sure you will read many different examples of how God has rescued people from appalling circumstances in this book. Now here is my testimony! I got born again at the age of eleven at a Billy Graham crusade in Birmingham in the 1980s and since then, I have lived for God wholeheartedly. I used to think because of that, my testimony was inferior to the guy who was supernaturally healed and so gave his life to the Lord, or the woman who had a near-death experience, or the youth saved out of addiction, until I realized this: it's good to never have had to go through these things in the first place. By God's grace, that was me and I thank him for it.

You see, it is not just about what we are saved from as Christians, it's more about what we are saved and called to. The title of this book and the scripture from which it is taken calls upon us to be able to give a reason for the hope we profess. People expect to hear not just what God has saved and delivered us from, they want to know what God can continue to do for them after they have turned their life over to him. So many people believe there is no significant reason to follow him. That is why many think 'Why should I live for God?' or 'I've got plenty of time and I can think about that when I'm older.' Like it or not, people are influenced by results and unfortunately the results they see from many Christians are indifferent to say the least. My encouragement to you is this: live for God with all your heart, mind and strength. Let him move on your behalf as you yield to him. As you do this, your life will speak in a way that will give your words greater credibility to those to whom you witness.

You may say, 'Well, how will my life speak?' It will speak through the way you treat your husband or wife, raise your kids, act at work, love people and worship your God. This is my testimony and this is to his glory. Remember, 'The end of a matter is better than its beginning' (Ecc. 7:8) so praise God for the miraculous testimony, but praise God for the life that speaks of his goodness, love and provision.

Gavin White

Gavin White is an elder and trustee of King's Church in Greater Manchester. He has responsibility for finance and administration within the church and has a heart and vision to help Christians 'make Jesus famous' in their communities, their workplaces and the world of politics. Gavin is married to Rachel and has two children.

'Christ in you, the hope of glory'. (Col. 1:27)

'Hope' is a short word but one that carries a wealth and depth of meaning and power. People of all faiths and none talk about 'having hope for the future' whether that is for their family, for their career or for their nation. Hope is a universal term that carries much power when you find the true source from which it comes.

I became a Christian when I was eight years old. I grew up in an atmosphere of hope that was found in the gospel of Jesus Christ. My parents were passionate and committed Christians. Their lives pointed me to Jesus. However, I knew that I had to have this hope for myself. It soon dawned on me from a young age that I couldn't have a faith that was purely something I did by attending church or saying the right things. A true hope can never be just an external thing. This hope had to become living. It had to become part of who I was: it had to change my heart and my whole life.

I once saw the preacher Keri Jones show how, when a can of coke is empty, it can be very easily crushed. But when it is full, it is nearly impossible to crush. Our lives are similar to this. It's what happening on the inside that matters.

You may know that God is for you and he is with you, but until you know that he lives in you, you can be easily crushed. I was a very shy lad when I was growing up. I used to get discouraged quite easily by various things like not being able to swim or being short. God radically took hold of my life during my teenage years and not only showed how much he was for me, how he was with me and how he loved me – I also knew deep down that he lived in me by the powerful and living presence of Christ. Paul told the church in Colosse over two thousand years ago: 'Christ in you, the hope of glory'.

That's my reason for hope: 'Christ in me, the hope of glory'.

My reason for hope is not about me, it's about him. It's about Christ and how he has changed my life. Christ gives me a hope for my wife and my family. Christ gives me hope for the council estate where I live that is running pretty empty on hope. Christ gives me hope for our nation that has many other 'gods' like the Premier League or the National Lottery, but not the true 'God of Hope'.

The hope that is found in the Bible is one that faces facts, but stays in faith. It's one that dreams big but starts small. It's a hope that satisfies the soul but humbles the spirit. There is nothing lacking in the Christ in me. He is all that I need for a hope-filled life. There is never any deferred or failed hope in the kingdom of God. Jesus gives us hope and fulfils our dreams, bringing life to us in all its fullness. That's my reason for hope.

> 'Hope deferred makes the heart sick, but a longing fulfilled is a tree of life.' (Prov. 13:12)

Steve Clifford

Steve Clifford works as part of the Inspire/Pioneer network, is a member of the Soul Survivor leadership team and chairs the national Hope '08 initiative. He is part of Bless, an Inspire/Pioneer Church in West London. Steve is married to Ann and has two adult children.

So many reasons to lose hope.

I walk through the Kibera squatter camp in Nairobi, Kenya, and I am faced with a sea of humanity. The largest of such camps in Africa; almost a million people crammed into just a few acres, tens of thousands of kids running after you, wanting to make contact. The mud, the smell, open drains, refuse everywhere (all those wretched plastic bags). It's safe during the day, but not a good place to be wandering around at night.

I sit with my dear friends Ness and Rich, with Josiah their newly born child, less than a day old, drifting from life to death – so much care, so much love, yet Josiah is not with us today.

I remember the prayers that we prayed which don't seem to have been answered, the prophetic words that have been given but don't as yet seem to have been fulfilled.

There are the news reports of 9/11, 7/7, Iraq, Afghanistan and of course all the other wars and atrocities around the world which don't hit our broadcasts but are still as real as ever to those living through them.

Yet despite all this, deep down at the very core of my being, there is a sense that God has not given up on his world. That's hope. Where does that hope come from? For me it comes from what I can only describe as God-encounters and revelations which go back years now: I remember being seventeen years old, sitting in church hearing the story of Jesus, his life, his death, his coming back to life. I had heard it all before but somehow on that evening it made sense. Jesus wanted to be my Saviour and to become my friend. For me it was as if something switched on inside. You might call it faith or indeed maybe even hope. A few months later I sat in my bed-room, coming to a fresh revelation that God also wanted to be a Father to me – my own dad had died when I was five years old so that was a hard one. I could handle God as Lord, Creator, King of the universe – but Dad! Then of course there was later discovering the Spirit's availability to me, wanting not just to be with me but in me, an ever-present friend, enabling me to be the person God wanted me to be, equipping me for a life of service. All this adds up. There are loads of reasons to lose hope, but I still have hope. This hope often creeps up on me in the most surprising places, frequently in the little things of life: driving in my car early in the morning; listening to some music; seeing the sun rise; being aware that I am 'not on my own'.

At the meal table with a crowd of friends we laugh and joke and exchange stories and I realize that I was made for this.

A walk by the sea, a film, a special piece of music, ski-ing down the mountain with the sun in the sky, the snow beneath my feet, my family around me . . . and of course there are the answers to prayer, 'when coincidences appear to happen more often after I have prayed'.

Even when things seem so dark, sitting in the hospital room with Ness and Rich, as Josiah died, there was an incredible awareness of the presence of God. We weren't on our own; God was with us in our pain, grief, disappointment and unanswered prayers. Hope was to be found even there.

Two

Politicians and
Civil Servants

Baroness Caroline Cox

Baroness Cox always says she is a nurse and a social scientist by intention and a baroness by astonishment. Appointed to the House of Lords in 1982, she cherishes the opportunity to speak in the parliamentary arena for those who cannot speak for themselves. Baroness Cox is the CEO of Humanitarian Aid Relief Trust (HART).

I have the privilege of spending much of my time with oppressed people in many parts of the world, not served by major aid organizations for political or security reasons. Many of these victims of persecution are Christians. We in HART return from visiting them inspired by their faith, courage, dignity and miracles of grace.

One example is Bishop, just elected Archbishop, Benjamin Kwashi and his wife Gloria, of the Diocese of Jos, Nigeria. Last year, militants attacked his home, to kill him. He was away, so they battered one of his sons unconscious. They tortured Gloria in indescribable ways and beat her so badly that she lost her eyesight (now restored). On his return, Bishop Ben sent an amazing message, describing how he had visited Gloria in hospital. She was out of intensive care, able to receive Holy Communion. They prayed, worshipped, laughed and praised God that they had been found worthy to suffer for his kingdom. They also prayed that all Gloria's pain, humiliation and anguish would be used by God to strengthen his Church.

When we saw Bishop Ben last year, he challenged us

> We have a faith worth living for and it is a faith worth dying for. So do not compromise our faith.

When we have such beacons of hope in a faith they are ready to die for, they not only give us a 'reason for hope'. They challenge us not to betray their hope and I pray we will not fail them.

Colonel Robin Vickers

*Robin Vickers is a British Army officer of twenty-nine years'
service. Having completed ten and a half months in Baghdad
he is currently serving in the Ministry of Defence in
Whitehall. Robin is married with two sons.*

As an Army officer I have spent much time in troubled
parts of the world: Northern Ireland, Bosnia, Sierra
Leone and, most recently, Iraq. In each of these situations I have stood alongside people facing extremely
challenging circumstances: the threat of hunger, home-
lessness, disease and physical danger. Facing such deprivation, it has been humbling and inspiring to see so
many holding on to hope, believing, against all odds,
that their lot will improve. Such examples as these make
me ever more determined to hold on to the hope to
which I have been called as a Christian.

In the summer of 1998 in Bosnia-Herzegovina I met a
family that had fled the atrocities of ethnic cleansing.
This cleansing took place between fellow villagers, long-
term friends and neighbours, who happened to belong
to another ethnic group. It is incredible this can happen
in modern Europe. The father was a former professor of
history. He and his family had walked from the western
edge of the country to its eastern border with their world
in a wheelbarrow, thinking to start afresh. Two years on,
this man (who had become a forester in the mean time)
had to flee once again, with his family carrying whatever they could between them. Surrounded again by

violent sectarianism, Bosnian-Serbs were no longer safe. The family made its way back into Bosnia to Banja Luka in the west of the country. On arrival in the city they met by chance someone who'd had his own home partially destroyed in the sectarian war. He lent this shell of a house to the family. Soon after this some British soldiers, including me, discovered them and offered what help they could to prepare the house for the onset of winter. The striking aspect of the tale was their determination to eventually rebuild their lives in their original village several miles further west and to forgive their Croat neighbours for what had happened. The bravery of these people gives me hope that it is possible to rise above all life's experiences – however terrible – to reach something better.

A year after the conclusion of a bloody rebel war in Sierra Leone I was sent there as part of a UN mission. The mission was to help rebuild this West African state. Devastated by a war inspired by greed for power and control of mineral resources – particularly the infamously named 'blood diamonds' – the country was in great need of assistance from other nations.

I made contact with Barbara, an English woman, who had gone to Sierra Leone a decade earlier to work as a secretary for a non-governmental organization (NGO). Then she met the pupils of the Melton Margai School for the Blind in Freetown: and gave up everything to serve these children. Because of their blindness, they had been abandoned by their families. Surviving the horrors of two violent rebel attacks, she remained committed to this work, calling on everyone she met – me included – to help out and publicize the work of the school.

One day, in Freetown, two colleagues and I were searching for the remains of the national railway workshops when we came upon a makeshift refugee camp. There were twelve thousand people there and it had been forgotten or overlooked by the UN aid agencies, something we were able to correct immediately. This random discovery reminded me that our loving Father had not forgotten these people.

I joined a Sierra Leonean church of some five hundred members. These special people had nothing in worldly terms but were rich in thankfulness and praise for what little they did have. Memories of such colourful and exuberant worship will remain with me forever.

And so to Baghdad, just a year ago, where I also found many reasons to hope. Though living just one mile from Sadr City (the part of Baghdad that has experienced and originated more violence than most other parts of Iraq) and working each day in the infamous Ministry of Interior I had the opportunity to meet inspiring and courageous Iraqis and others too from the international community. Though many were threatened with or had experienced attacks or kidnapping because of their family name, tribal affiliation, or religion, they still risked all to come to work, believing this was the only way to build a future for their loved ones and for their country. A number became friends and confidants, assisting me in making sense of complex situations and enabling me to direct help from the international coalition. One year on things do appear somewhat better, and certainly the daily diet of great violence that prevailed in 2006–07 has lessened. The courage, sacrifice, and friendliness of these Iraqis – who come from each of the major religious groups of the country – and my brave colleagues have changed my preconceptions. Furthermore it encourages me to believe that in all difficulties, from the international to the personal, something good can be shaped.

The indomitable spirit of all these people dares me to believe it possible that the God of all hope *will* 'fill you with all joy and peace' (Rom. 15:13).

Michael Foster MP

Michael Foster is the Labour MP for Hastings and Rye. His political interests include child poverty, pensioner issues and animal welfare. Previously a solicitor, he lives in Hastings with his wife Rosemary.

When it comes to hope I think MPs must be experts. In the 1992 election Hastings and Rye was won by a Tory and the Labour candidate was 17,000 votes behind. In 1997, if I hadn't had hope I wouldn't have dared to contest the seat – but I did, and we won.

Hope helps us all to go that extra mile and to work just that extra bit harder to achieve our goals.

I recall my recent visit to the town of Hastings in Sierra Leone (with which we are now twinned). The English Hastings has important challenges in terms of poverty and deprivation: but these pale into insignificance when compared to a town there – one of the poorest countries in Africa.

From our first day it was clear a huge gulf exists between our two societies. Every car journey began with the driver praying for the safe delivery of his passengers: hardly surprising when there are barely any road signs and the road is marked with frequent potholes.

We witnessed great material poverty and great suffering. Yet my abiding memory is the cheerfulness and energy that everyone, especially the children, possessed. They certainly had hope for their future even though there was little that could be called 'hopeful' in their lives.

My belief is that God has a great plan for all of us and that if we have hope then we will have the right outlook to enable us to do what is needed. And, just as importantly, we owe it to others who have hope but need help – like the citizens of Hastings, Sierra Leone – to reach out to them and attempt to make their hopes become a reality.

Rt. Hon. Ann Widdecombe MP

Ann Widdecombe was elected Member of Parliament in 1987. She has held numerous positions including Minister of State at the Department of Employment and the Home Office, and Shadow Home Secretary. Miss Widdecombe has written several novels. She frequently appears on television and radio.

My hope is for the unborn who, because they are unseen, have no rights. In 1937, in an age before incubators and antibiotics, a woman gave birth to twins in Gibraltar. They were two months premature and one was stillborn while the other was paralysed. Today there would be all manner of debate about the 'viability' of the paralysed baby. Ten years later the same woman was pregnant again and contracted German measles at the height of the danger period. The doctor was terrified the child would be born handicapped and today the pressure to abort would have been immense.

The paralysed baby was not paralysed for long and is now seventy years old, an enthusiastic and successful evangelical vicar and canon of the Church of England with children and grandchildren of his own. He is my brother. I am the child born, fit and healthy, after a pregnancy which included rubella and the woman was, of course, my mother.

My brother and I are alive because we were both conceived and born in an age when death was not seen as an answer to possible handicap. Today unborn children are scanned as part of a search and destroy mission

which has little to distinguish it from Hitler's T4 programme except his victims were born and today's are
unborn. May God forgive us.

Yet the mood is changing and in that lies my hope.
Photographic science has made people much more
aware that what is in the womb is not just a lump of tis-
sue but a recognisable, developing human being. Poll
after poll shows that the population believes there are
too many abortions and that many of them are occurring
too late. At last consciences are being stirred.

When my mother was old and frail she once told me
that she would see her stillborn son in heaven. I hope
she has.

Lord Alton of Liverpool

Married with four children, Lord David Alton was a member of the House of Commons for eighteen years and today is an Independent Crossbench Life Peer. Lord Alton is co-founder of the Jubilee Campaign, was treasurer of the All Party Pro-Life Group, and is a member of the bio-ethics committee appointed by the Catholic Bishops of England and Wales. He is the author of seven books.

I was born the product of a mixed marriage: English Anglican and Irish Catholic, and brought up in a period when there was still a lot of sectarian hatred. In my adopted city of Liverpool this frequently spilled over in the political and cultural life of the city.

The day after I was elected to the House of Commons in 1979, the Shadow Northern Ireland Secretary, Airey Neave, was killed by a car bomb as he left the House of Commons car park. It was part of a campaign of sectarian violence that has killed around four thousand people, injured thousands and has caused damage to the property and lives of countless others.

I don't think any of us expected to see the day when leaders from both sides of the divide, particularly Dr Ian Paisley and Martin McGuinness, would meet together to try and find a new way forward. But that is exactly what has happened, with both these influential leaders becoming the First Minister and Deputy Minister of Northern Ireland.

The Bible tells us that if a house is divided against itself, it cannot stand. When we are divided by sectarian hatred and when Christian allegiances end up becoming part of a tribalistic battle, it doesn't give much hope to the rest of the world. But the experience of Northern Ireland, where people have been willing to reach out and overcome their differences, shows that seemingly impossible obstacles can be overcome.

For the past few years, I have travelled on behalf of the Jubilee Campaign to places like the Democratic Republic of Congo, where four million have died, to southern Sudan where two million have died and, most recently, to Darfur where between two and four hundred thousand have been killed and over two million have been displaced.

In these and other places I have visited, like North Korea, Burma and the Middle East, there are terrible divisions between communities and seemingly intractable problems. In apparently hopeless situations like these, I feel that we can take encouragement and hope from what has happened in Northern Ireland.

My mother used to repeat an old Irish saying: 'It's better to light a candle than it is to curse the darkness.' As with Pandora's box, sometimes the only thing we are left with is hope. We must never lose it.

Three

Grassroots Folk

Steve Cattell

Steve Cattell, once a prolific criminal, now helps and supports people trapped in a lifestyle of addiction, including crime. He works throughout the UK giving talks in a variety of contexts. The head of Elim once told him to 'stay with the doors God opens, as no one will reach them like you can' and that's what he is doing. His book Unbreakable *has just been published.*

I was born into a life without love. I felt unwanted by my parents and rejected by my brothers. I felt hurt and angry. As I grew up I felt more anger and more hate. I was misunderstood by parents, teachers and neighbours and I withdrew. Crime became my release. Through crime I discovered a high I couldn't get elsewhere. I was ten years old when I was first locked in a cell. It marked the start of a total of twenty-four years in prison. Surviving inside meant becoming immune to everyone and everything. I would fight at every opportunity: other inmates, prison officers, the system that kept me from my beloved crime. The criminal world was a dark one but one which welcomes me. At night in the isolation units I would scream and pray to the devil to give me enough hate and enough anger to see me through until the next night. I didn't care about anyone. I became an armed robber, a drug dealer, and Britain's most prolific burglar: breaking into eight thousand homes a year. I'd marry and get my wife pregnant just to reduce my sentences, I'd rob my children of their father, my wife of her husband, and I didn't care.

I had once done some jobs with a heroin addict and he started talking to me about God. He'd managed to come off drugs and he'd gone straight. He said it was down to Jesus Christ. I thought he was mad, and I told him so, but he wouldn't leave me alone. He was constantly ringing me and praying for me and talking about a new way of life, a life of truth and hope. He said that the truth would set me free. I saw freedom in terms of being locked in a cell or not. I didn't realize that I was just as much a prisoner outside the prison walls as inside. I was a slave to crime. I had sentences hanging over me. He kept ringing me. I was desperate. I started to question whether there was any truth in God. It didn't make sense. If he was real, where was he when I was growing up? And if he knew my past how could he love me? How could he forgive me for the things I'd done? But things began to change, I began to feel love for the wife and family I'd treated so badly. I found myself confessing to police. I lost the desire to burgle and to hurt. I even stated to trust again, in God. I began to understand that through Christ I was a new creation.

It's been a steep learning curve. I've discovered that some Christians are suspicious of ex-convicts. I felt God calling me to reach out to people but there were so many barriers. I missed a lot of my education being in and out of institutions and churches and prisons sometimes mistrusted me – but I learned that God is in control. I now talk in prisons, colleges and churches. I have been interviewed for newspapers, radio and television. I even work with the police. With people this would be impossible, but not with God. My God is a God who opens doors. He is my dad. I trust him in everything.

Andrew Swift

Andrew Swift runs a supply chain consultancy and attends River Church, Maidenhead where he is part of the worship team and co-ordinates a small group. He is married and has two daughters.

'I know, I know, I know, that there is a God.'

These are the words of a song from the gospel singer Carman. More importantly, these words are instilled in my heart and came from the firm foundations my parents gave me.

Some may argue that my reason for hope is simply a belief set in my mind from years of church. But the truth I have isn't just in my mind – it's a part of me, in my mind, soul and heart – it's a deep certainty that I know the truth.

I have many memories of church. As a young lad I remember helping Dad collect water containers from a local college for use at the Good News Crusade camp. I remember sitting with him in preparation for my baptism when I was six years old. We had family times every week, creating a scrapbook as we made early discoveries about Jesus and we read inspiring books about missionaries doing God's work around the world. These are special childhood memories of God being the centre of my family life that I treasure and try to bring to my own young family now.

As I left home and went to university in the north-east my passion and zeal for God continued. I found secondary school to be academically challenging and was placed in the lower sets. I chose not to let this define me. Since then God has blessed me with passion and an entrepreneurial character. I have had my ups and downs, but God has never left my side. God has been there when I set up my first business, a surf shop in Leeds, and he directed my path as I moved down south to start my consultancy business. When I look back I can see he has been with me and I know this will continue to be true in my future.

There have been milestones in my life; you will read later how Rod and Ruthie Gilbert call these 'hope stones'. For me these stones are special memories, lost dreams, trials, and wisdom and understanding gained; all of them have been like the North Star, directing me to find my hope in Jesus. This hope says we will live in heaven and have the peace of an eternity with God. I know that God has started a good work in me which he will see through to completion.

I recently heard someone say that our struggle and wrestle with sin is only a positive reflection that God is working in our lives, for without God in our lives there would not be a struggle at all. The Light wrestles with our darkness! I can say that I have wrestled: nevertheless my future is secure. I know where I am heading: home, to be with my maker.

I always remember a great quote on the back of the book *Worship* by Bryn Jones. It said that all too often people struggle with finding the will or purpose of God in their life, but the thing that blesses God the most are people who worship him. This is what I pursue, to be foremost a worshipper of God, in the open at church as well as behind closed doors.

This book has become another blessing in my life as we have seen this project through to completion. I know my gifting is as a 'starter' and not a 'finisher' in projects.

But God has blessed this project from the start to the finish.

Who knows what God has in store for me in the future? Here am I, use me, is all I can pray. My destination is decided, my hope clear, but my journey is still being written. If he can do this in me, a person in whom teachers gave up hope, God can do this for you. I want to bring the hope I have found in Jesus not just to the unsaved but also to the church. Many people in churches across the world feel despondent and disillusioned, because they still need to find this hope in God. This hope is for everyone.

I want to help others discover this hope that I have found. It is this hope that causes me to sing of God's great love for the world.

Anne Raftery

Anne Raftery qualified as a teacher when she was twenty-one and taught at a primary school. She stayed at home to bring up her three daughters and later returned to work in schools as a support assistant for children with special needs. Her role has recently developed, giving her the opportunity to teach again and also have a pastoral role within the school community.

When I was young, I was what you might call 'a born worrier'; it seemed almost inherent in my personality. I was insecure and even though I had been brought up in a Christian home and believed in the Lord Jesus from an early age, I was always an anxious person. I remember a friend at college saying to me, 'You must enjoy worrying because you do it all the time!'

Yes, I was one of those people who, even if there was nothing to worry about, would always find something. I didn't realize at that stage of my life, the full extent of all that Jesus had won for me on the cross, nor how deep and faithful is his love for me.

In my final year at college, feeling empty after my boyfriend of two years (someone I had known from childhood) finished with me, I joined the Christian Union. It was there, amongst that lovely fellowship of vibrant Christians, that I first experienced the power of the Holy Spirit in my life and began composing songs out of the new-found joy in my heart. The change had begun, but it still took many years of the Lord's patience and nurturing to bring me to the place where I could, at last, give all my cares and anxieties to him and leave them there. I began to realize that my worrying was evidence of my lack of trust in God's sovereignty and faithfulness. I prayed earnestly for God to take me deeper and secure me 'in him' and as the years have gone by he has been faithfully doing this.

When I look back at my life, I am so grateful for all that God has done for me: the godly people who have touched my life and caused me to say in my heart, 'If only I could be like them'; the times of loneliness which caused my heart to cry out to him; the sad and confusing times that made me rely more on him; for family and friends, all of whom, whether Christian or not, have taught me things about myself which have led me closer to God; and most of all, the realization that he's been watching over me since I was conceived in my mother's womb and drawing me to himself throughout all my life experiences.

How wonderful is God's love and faithfulness.

> Cast all your anxiety on him because he cares for you. (1 Pet. 5:7)

> Do not be anxious about anything, but in everything, by prayer and petition, with thanksgiving, present your request to God. And the peace of God, which transcends all understanding, will guard your hearts and your minds in Christ Jesus. (Phil. 4:6,7)

Jonathan Davis

Jonathan Davis owns Paradise Gardens, a busy gardening and landscaping company. He has a passion to pray and see people healed by the power of God. Jonathan is married to Heather and lives in Berkshire.

I fought Post-Viral Chronic Fatigue Syndrome (also known as M.E.) for many years. In common with many sufferers I was continually exhausted and had blurred vision, insomnia and a host of other complaints.

In the autumn of 2005, after nearly five years of it, Heather and I were reaching the point of absolute frustration. We had paid for private medical treatment to try to get some results. I had developed the illness shortly after our wedding so for almost the whole of our marriage the illness had challenged us, especially financially. We had come a long way, and were stronger for it – but we struggled to see a way forward.

I had not worked properly for three years: my prospects were not promising. Over the years we had known God's goodness through our friends and local church. We could see his handprint on our journey and we knew the reality of his love.

In 2004, I had had a real sense of God speaking to me, telling me that good things would happen in the following year, but something of far greater value would happen in 2006. In 2005 I started to work part-time but a few months later had to leave due to a relapse.

Despite feeling discouraged, a recent quote I had heard had stuck with me. It changed my whole outlook on Chronic Fatigue. It came from Bill Johnson, a pastor in Redding, California. He talked of hope as 'the joyful anticipation of good things'.

In this time of seeking answers from God I asked for hope. No sooner than I did so, I experienced a real, tangible hope. I found I could not get depressed about my situation. I was not well, but I had hope that something good would happen.

The new year dawned, and with it, the opportunity to visit Redding Church. With all my medication, nutritional supplements and energy drinks I and a group from our church flew to California.

This church had been experiencing regular medically certifiable healings for a number of years. My trip was a bid to say to myself, to God and to others, that my condition was not going to beat me. If I had to live a restricted life forever, I would do that. If I did not get healed, it would not change my view of God: he could still heal me any time and he wanted to do so – my time would come. Either way I would get on with my life.

One of the guys at Redding offered to pray for me and see me healed there and then. I sat down and he prayed out loud to God to heal in Jesus' name.

A heat passed through my head and down my body. As it came into my head it was as if all the parts of my brain that were so dysfunctional and out of sync clicked back into place, like cogs in a clock beginning to work again. I sneaked a look across the room in case anyone was watching and the heat was my embarrassment. No one so much as blinked but everything came into sharp focus.

One of the symptoms of Chronic Fatigue is endless exhaustion. As the heat passed down into my body, I felt as if a huge bottomless pit inside me had been blocked up. I knew I would never be that tired ever again.

It all happened in the space of a few minutes. As a test of this 'God experience' I decided to stop taking my many pills and supplements. I have not taken them again. Today I am well, and remain so.

I am still hopeful: to raise a family; for my business to grow; and to see many people made well by God's power. You too can be made well. I invite you to join me today in seeking a greater presence of his love in your life: there is so much goodness in him.

Leon Sinani

Leon Sinani is from Kosovo. He came to England as a refugee and is now studying network engineering. In his spare time he loves playing football and listening to hip-hop.

As foreign lands and seas passed beneath the plane, I dreamt of what my country might look like. Would there be homes, parks, green fields, laughter and children playing? Would there be peace? Or would there still be war, death and poverty? I hoped for beauty but my memories of war still haunted me from when I was last there. How had my homeland changed in the ten years since I left as a refugee?

I walked and walked, and although the countryside was still beautiful, gradually I saw the reality of what the war had left behind: houses carried the physical marks of war and people were impoverished. It brought sadness to my heart: but the sadness turned to hope as I realized God could use me to change these people's lives. I imagined bringing my British friends to help me bring hope to Kosovo.

Back in the UK, I told my friends at school and at church about the reality there – about the poor and about how a small amount of money could have a big impact. We formed a group called 'Hope in Kosovo' and started fundraising for £2000. (I wasn't surprised when my sponsored silence was a big earner.) Then with the money raised, we returned to Kosovo to invest it.

Every day we visited different homes. We would sit down and chat with people, discovering their pressing needs. We went to a massive warehouse to buy all the families needed such as mattresses, flour, sugar, salt, washing powder, toys and oil. We had enough money to help seven families, providing enough food to last them the year. However, we were giving them more than food: we were showing people that we cared and that God cared. As we left, one man said to us, 'If it hadn't been for you guys I would not have seen hope shine through.'

Next year, when I'm sixteen, I plan to return with more friends and more money so that we can share our precious hope.

Cathy Lyden

Cathy Lyden is a PE teacher from Scotland. She works at a secondary school in Hull. Cathy has a heart for evangelism and is actively involved in her local church, training 'the body' in this area and trying to reach the lost in her community.

Ever seen someone give their life to Christ and wondered 'How genuine is it?' Ever had a conversation with a non-Christian friend or family member and heard that voice which says 'They're not the type to become a Christian.' Ever prayed for someone's salvation and thought, 'Is this making a difference?' For every person who just nodded, here's your reason for hope . . .

I was brought up in a Catholic family. I loved going to church and I gave up chocolate every Lent. I loved God. Now, this isn't another one of those stories that goes 'Oh, I just slipped away from church.' No, I made a solid, conscious decision at the age of fourteen to turn 180 degrees in the opposite direction from God. Why?

When I was growing up my mum always seemed to be at church; every single night of the week, she'd come in from work, dump her bags and then I'd hear 'OK, I'm off to church.' A couple of hours later she'd return. This continued for months and years and I began to resent the time God got to spend with her. One night, I just asked her straight out 'Who do you love more, me or God?' With little hesitation her word like a spear through my heart, she replied 'God'. That was it. That was the moment I turned on my heels.

I hated God. I was a real 'Paul' of the twentieth century. So when my elder brother returned from university one year to say he had become a born-again Christian I was unimpressed to say the least. He did the whole, 'Repent, you need God, he loves you' repertoire and I rejected it more violently with every syllable. He persisted, as did I. My brother got to the point of realizing that conversations with me were futile and that all he could do was pray.

He persistently prayed for two years despite me showing no signs of change. And on 9 October 2002 he sat in his flat in Edinburgh with fourteen of his friends still holding his request before the Lord. In Liverpool his prayers were being answered.

God knows me pretty well. And he knew at the time that if I were going to listen to anyone about God, it would need to be in the form of a tall, handsome athletic figure. The figure was named Dan. The night in question, he didn't tell me anything I didn't already know. In fact he didn't tell me anything, he asked the one question no one thought to ask me, 'Why do you hate God so much?' As I contemplated the truth behind the answer, tears rolled down my face. The tight steel vice that had surrounded my hardened and bitter heart for years began to loosen. I confessed my hurt to God and he filled me with his love.

It truly was my road-to-Damascus moment. How could this person who hated God so much, who rejected so fiercely the words of the gospel now be crying out for forgiveness?

Quite soon after my conversion I moved away, and I am no longer in touch with Dan. But I sometimes think 'Does he ever wonder if I am still walking with God?' Well, I am, and walking stronger than ever. You see, when God saves, it's always genuine. When we think

there's a type who becomes a Christian, God says anyone can come. And when we pray and think is it really
making a difference, *believe*, because it is. Whenever I
doubt, I remember that there is absolutely no way I got
here by myself: only God could have turned me, a
Christian-hater, into a mad evangelist. He saved me and
he saved me for a purpose. So where is my hope? In him.

" . . . For I know the plans I have for you," declares the
LORD, "plans to prosper you and not to harm you, plans
to give you hope and a future." (Jer. 29:11)

John Swift

John Swift has worked as an Environmental Health Practitioner for nearly forty years. He is a local voluntary community mediator and the trustee of a small international children's charity. He is married to Joy and they have four children and two grandchildren.

The adage 'God has no grandchildren; he only has children' has been variously ascribed to evangelists Billy Graham, Luis Palau and David du Plessis. As a boy growing up in a Christian home, I was aware that I needed to have a personal faith and trust in the Lord Jesus and that I couldn't live off the faith of my parents. So at an early age I committed my life to Christ. I can still recall the incredible lightness and joy which flooded my young life at that moment.

Personal experiences cannot be the sole reason for hope. I have a hope in the truth of the Bible, a hope that Jesus is who he says he is and that you can have a day-by-day relationship with God, a hope in an eternal life which goes on past physical death and a hope that this old world will be put right in the end.

It is sad to say but my hope in these things has been threatened more by the behaviour of 'church folk' and theologians than by unbelievers or the challenge of other faiths. However, faith and hope cannot be absorbed by osmosis and my own certainty of hope has come from a personal pursuit of God through the Scriptures and being exposed to evidence of God working in people's lives.

The Bible presents to me a satisfactory explanation of life, a God who is not remote and who demonstrates his love to the human race in a manner which could not be conceived of by any science fiction writer. I feel I can trust what it says and when we put it into practice it works for the everyday issues of life.

As one gets older you realize that no one really has it all together, we are all in the process of being changed to become more like Jesus. My hope is founded on the God of love who not only reveals himself in the Bible but also has reached out to ordinary people and has extended mercy and grace to us, sometimes in extraordinary ways.

A final reason for my hope in Christ is the effects of the pervasive hopelessness and futility I see around me in a society which has rejected this hope.

For me the physical regeneration of our cities and towns, attempts to raise educational standards, reduce poverty and improve health measures will achieve little – unless there is a restoration of hope and purpose which Jesus brings.

Four

Entertainment

Sir Cliff Richard

Having celebrated his fiftieth anniversary in the music business in 2008, Sir Cliff Richard is indisputably Britain's all-time greatest hit-maker. With 121 hits, he has been in the UK charts for over twenty years. Sir Cliff has also been involved in films, musicals, concert tours and television shows.

It was a few years into my show-business career when I first sensed a sort of incompleteness. I don't know how else to put it. It was as though there was something more to life, despite the fact that I had so much going for me – certainly as much fame, fortune and popularity as any person could handle. The girls screamed, the hits came regularly, accountants were employed to cope with the income, but, despite all that, it didn't add up to satisfaction. When I went home and took off the public mask, I still had to live with the real me. I knew that success, fans and money were no compensation for being restless deep inside.

It was a while before I really understood the reason for this restlessness and for literally years, I kept up the barrage of questions and argument. Looking back, I'm grateful that there were those around me who could not only answer the questions but who also put God's love into practice. Actions always speak louder than words, and somehow I saw in their lives what was patiently and repeatedly explained to me: 'For God so loved the world that he gave his one and only Son, that whoever believes in him shall not perish but have eternal life' (Jn. 3:16).

I knew my life wasn't right and I wanted to change. I accepted that Jesus' death was somehow the key to it all and, what's more, I believed that Jesus wasn't a dusty character from history. Dead people might still have some influence, but they don't change lives. And I had little intellectual difficulty in believing that Jesus was, in some miraculous way, still alive.

I started that commitment, and I discovered a new lifestyle, when I lay on my bed at night in the mid-1960s and prayed very simply that Jesus would come into the life of Cliff Richard and save it and rule over it. Now the things I believed with my head had extended to my heart and my life. Jesus' words in the last book of the Bible focused it for me. Revelation 3:20 says 'Here I am! I stand at the door and knock. If anyone hears my voice and opens the door, I will come in and eat with him, and he with me.'

After my prayer there were no dramas, no flashing lights or booming voices – just a quiet sense of peace and a hint of excitement. Now, more than forty years later, the peace is deeper and the excitement is greater.

Mike Rimmer

Mike Rimmer is a broadcaster and journalist with the BBC and Cross Rhythms. He's an expert commentator on the Christian music scene. Mike is married to Pippa and they belong to Church Alive in Birmingham where they serve on the leadership team.

I was seventeen years old and I was delivering newspapers in Newcastle upon Tyne. Every evening, I would pass by a student house where some girls lived. They'd smile and occasionally chat to me. They seemed friendly enough so one rainy June evening I somehow invited myself in for a coffee. I knew the girls in the house were Christians because they had a sticker on the window that proudly proclaimed 'New Life in Jesus'. Even though they were in the God squad I wasn't put off because, well, they were girls right?

My seventeen-year-old self was a typical teenager. I was a bit insecure, I was mad about music and I was busy having a good time with my mates. I was also doing a pretty good job of failing my A Level courses . . . but I was having fun. I had a huge social life with a number of different social circles and was never short of a party or a gig to go to at weekends. I would roll home at dawn on a Sunday morning after a good night out and climb into bed – and yet when I woke up for Sunday lunch, I would lie in bed staring at the ceiling, wondering if was more? No matter how good the party, how great the gig, there would still be a time when I was on my own staring at the ceiling, feeling empty.

I was born two months early and back in the sixties, that was a big deal. I was placed in an incubator and the nurses asked my father if he wanted the last rites said over me because I wasn't going to make it. Of course I did make it but my dad, being from good atheist stock, was appalled at the question. His religious convictions were that if his sons were to find God, it would be up to us. Consequently I had no church background, never went to Sunday school and had no idea about religion. I would probably have been best described as an agnostic. I just wasn't convinced there was anything out there . . . but then I hadn't really been looking.

The student girls in their house had been looking. They were Christians and they had spotted the paperboy walking past each evening and had started praying for me. They even got their friends to pray for me as well. I had no clue that I was the subject of people's personal prayers, but when I walked into their home, their warmth struck me. I couldn't put my finger on it, but they were unlike anybody I had ever met. They were full of life and fun, and had a bubbling joy I'd not encountered in any of my friends. They were the first Christians I had known and I was immediately intrigued.

Over dinner, I asked provocative things about their faith and told them that there was no way I could ever believe in Christianity unless it was scientifically proven. During the next few days I hung out with them in the evenings, met their boyfriends, and thought about the stuff we were talking about. Inevitably we talked about God stuff and it was the first time anybody had explained things to me. A couple of days later my grandmother died. She was the only person close to me to pass away. It shook me up and I had an early reminder of my own mortality. I had no concept of the afterlife, but her death made me think about the emptiness of my life. Even though I had spent a great deal of energy trying to fill it, the dull ache during the morning after wouldn't leave me.

I'd first walked into the girls' house on a wet Wednesday night. The following Sunday I was alone in my bedroom, thinking about what they'd been saying to me for the past five days. They'd given me some verses from the Bible to read: I decided to look them up. I sat in silence thinking that although I didn't understand everything, I wanted what they had. I wanted the sense of life and purpose that spilled out of their words and actions and so I prayed for the first time. I didn't know how to pray so it wasn't very grand. It went along the lines of, 'OK God, if you're there, I realize I've done stuff that hurt you and I want to change. I want what those girls have got so will you come into my life and help me?' I sat in silence and waited to see what would happen.

There were no flashing lights but there was a gentle feeling of peace. Something tangible happened at that moment that was so real, the feeling has stayed with me ever since. It was like God walked into the room and put his arms around me. I still didn't understand how much he loved me but I'd made my first step. God had moved into the void in my life and taken up residence and he's never left. Thirty years later, life has thrown its fair share of rubbish at me, there have been good times and bad, but God has never left. He's made all the difference, helped me through the bad and celebrated the good with me.

It all started when some girls prayed for me and chose to tell me about Jesus. Now I'm doing the same for you. Take the first step. Jesus won't disappoint you.

Mark Stevens

Mark Stevens, born in Hobart, Tasmania, was a cast member of the Australian soap Neighbours. *He now lives in Bradford with his wife.*

From a young age I had a great love and passion for music and would often record myself singing on my grandfather's portable cassette player. This love for music carried on right through my school years. At the age of twelve, I started piano lessons and soon after my parents bought me a piano. By the age of thirteen I was writing my own songs. With one of these songs I played in a 'Talent Quest' where I won the Encouragement Award and soon after that I won the talent show.

There were some judges at the Talent Quest who were producers of the biggest kids' show in Australia *Young Talent Time*. My mother and I were flown from Tasmania to Melbourne where I auditioned for it. In front of producers and directors I sang my heart out and was stopped halfway through my second song and asked to join the show. For me to be a part of the show would be a massive decision for my parents because it would uproot the whole family from Tasmania to Melbourne. The show was aired every Saturday night on prime time television. It had a viewing audience of one million people, which is huge in Australia with its population of twenty million.

I was catapulted out of a life of obscurity into a life where everybody knew my name. I could not venture outside without being followed by hordes of kids who were avid fans of the show. This was kind of difficult for a kid of thirteen years to handle. We were required to go to school as any normal child would – however, the life we were leading was far from normal. We were doing concert tours that stood us in front of fifteen thousand people every night, sometimes for months. I was tormented at school by bullies. I was beaten up on the street and called all kinds of names. I just thought this was all part and parcel of what could be expected. So at the age of sixteen I employed a full-time bodyguard. The violence I was subjected to caused me to withdraw and play truant. I began to drink, smoke cigarettes and marijuana and 'escape' from reality. I became quite violent at school and was expelled from high school for beating up a guy who verbally abused me.

Soon after my seventeenth birthday I decided to find myself a good agent who could help me further my music career. I felt I needed to move on from the show and try something different. Instead of a singing audition, my agent found me an acting audition for *Neighbours*, an Australian soap opera hugely popular around the world. I auditioned for the part of a young tearaway called 'Nick Page'. I won the part and began work on the show. I was working with Kylie Minogue, Jason Donovan, Craig McLaughlin (Henry), Alan Dale (Jim), Ian Smith (Harold) and other household names.

Now on the flip side of all this was a young man who was desperate for some kind of meaning to this thing called life. I was born a soul searcher, a deep thinker. I don't know if it was because I was an arty, creative person but I was deeply curious to find answers to the bigger questions of 'Why are we here?' and 'What is the meaning of all this?' I had lived a life of fame and fortune from a young age and it hadn't filled the void within me.

I tried to find answers in relationships with women, but couldn't. I tried to fill the void with alcohol and drugs, but couldn't . . . By the age of eighteen I was famous, yet my personal life was becoming more and more messed up. I was snorting cocaine, taking drugs, smoking and sleeping around – and I was a full-blown alcoholic.

My time on *Neighbours* came to an end so I decided to move to England to record an album. I had just signed a record deal with BMG/RCA and had signed with a well-known manager in Australia by the name of Glenn Wheatley. Whilst in England I worked in pantomime, recorded an album and promoted the album throughout the country. I was earning thousands of pounds every week and spending it almost as quickly as I was earning it. I thought this lifestyle would last forever.

Progressively my alcohol and drug addictions became worse. I was drunk most of the time and was high on drugs nearly as much. I would turn up to recording sessions late or not at all. People who were investing their time, money and energy in me began to not take me seriously. After three to four years of this lifestyle I had lost it all. I had blown all the money, I had sold everything I owned, I had become estranged from my family and I had become a wreck. My life was a mess.

I decided to return home to Tasmania and moved back in with my parents. I got work singing in dingy pubs in front of ten to fifteen people. I was out of it all of the time.

Then one day my brother turned up and said, 'Let's go back to England.' I didn't need to think twice as my parents' relationship was strained and Tasmania was the last place I wanted to be. My brother and I moved back and tried to get our music off the ground but I couldn't shake my addictions. They were so bad he moved back to Australia because he couldn't stay and watch me slowly kill myself. At this time I was living with an old friend who I had worked alongside during my time with BMG/RCA. She would bring home CDs from the record company and I would sell them so I could pay for a hit of heroin. I had hit rock bottom. I would get just enough money day-by-day to get me high and drunk.

One night I was in a club and I met a young lady who at the time was working for Michael Barrymore. She was an Australian and had watched me on TV as a kid. We became good friends and started to date each other. Because of my lifestyle, I messed her around and treated her badly. However she remained a friend. I didn't know it at the time but she was a Christian and after our relationship she had returned to church and got her life right with God. She and some of her friends began to pray for me and God began to reveal himself to me in a powerful way. I would have moments of peace and clarity that baffled me because my life was mostly lived in turmoil. When I was talking to people I would know things about them that were beyond the surface. I began to sense a real compassion for people and would spend hours talking to people for whom no one cared. I began to search deeper and deeper for true meaning and would find myself mentioning God to people and having conversations about God. This was so foreign to me because I had not grown up in a Christian home. God was working on me but I didn't understand it at the time.

The night my life changed, I was invited to a party at my ex-girlfriend's house. I turned up four hours late with my drug-dealer. My ex confronted me, 'What are you doing with your life?' I remember sliding down a wall and cupping my head in my hands and replying, 'I don't know any more. I think I need God.' I couldn't believe what had just come out of my mouth.

Later on I remember the room suddenly filling with the presence of God and I began to cry out to God, realizing that he had witnessed all of my actions, yet still loved me and wanted to help me. I cried and cried as God began to deal with the guilt and shame in my life and reveal his forgiveness for all the wrong I'd done. A few days later I also realized that all my addictions had disappeared. Even my filthy language was gone. I had met Jesus Christ and he had saved and rescued me from who I was. He began to show me who I truly was and reveal his plan and purpose for my life.

I sit here writing this eleven years later, so thankful for what God has done in my world. I have lived more, done more and been a part of some incredible things in the last eleven years. I am now happily married and I work full time at church and absolutely love what I do: assisting in heading up the music team. I'm active in the community, helping people who have lived a similar life to me. They have the same needs and want answers to the same questions. I have seen my family's lives changed. My mother became a Christian and so did my brother and his wife. God has been so good to me and it's just the beginning of an incredible journey. I haven't even started . . .

Cameron Stout

Cameron Stout is from Orkney. He won Channel 4's Big Brother *in 2003 and is a car fanatic and keen traveller.*

Hope is a curious thing, and very personal too. People's interpretations and expectations of it vary enormously. I know mine do, depending on what situation I'm in at a particular time.

'I hope I get this assignment submitted in time.'

'I hope the car makes it through the MOT.'

'I hope it's a nice day tomorrow.'

Some hopes are pretty glib, some have a lot more importance attached to them. Sometimes hopes are attached to a worry we have, when we're not sure how a particular situation will work out.

I want to tell you about a time when I was worried about something and I found a direct message of reassurance in the Bible.

Nearing the end of my stint in the *Big Brother* house, a situation arose which made me wonder if the producers' warnings about press intrusion and skewed reporting would actually come true. We had been asked serious questions about contentious issues, and I tried to answer as fully as I could, even on topics that I'd never discussed or thought much about previously.

At the back of my mind was the warning about how the media can interpret what's shown, and cast participants in a good or bad light depending on their mood of the moment. Would they take my views and Christian standpoint out of context and make me out to be something I'm not?

I had been Christian for more than twenty years and I knew some of the familiar scripture passages about hope – but I wanted something fresh this time. I love Psalms and turned to that book, coming across Psalm 91. You'd think that having been a Christian for so long, I would be quite familiar with it, but no – it was the first time I'd seen it, and I really believe God had kept it for me, for just that occasion.

The passage finishes up like this

> "Because he loves me," says the LORD, "I will rescue him;
> I will protect him, for he acknowledges my name.
> He will call upon me, and I will answer him;
> I will be with him in trouble,
> I will deliver him and honor him." (vv. 14–15)

Isn't that amazing? What more could I have hoped for!

Stephen Deal

Stephen Deal was the writer and director of Stripes Theatre Company and wrote the drama sketches for productions such as Burning Questions, Hopes and Dreams *and* Here and Now. *In addition, he has written for radio and television and has had several volumes of comedy sketches published. His material is performed in many countries around the world.*

I've been a writer since 1984, well, since about 1966 actually, but most of my early work was done in crayon and has not withstood the test of time. I graduated in 1984 and was faced with either finding employment or making my own. I'd recently found myself in a wheelchair thanks to a rare form of muscular dystrophy so I decided to pursue something that could be done sitting down. My degree in Religious Studies and Psychology left me with a choice between writing and psychoanalysing vicars, and since word processors had recently been invented . . .

One thing led to another and before long I was travelling the length and breadth of the land with a small Christian theatre company putting on shows in churches, schools and theatres, and working on missions and at festivals and conferences. All the while my condition was deteriorating. As I became physically weaker, and thus more dependent on the help of others it was as if God wanted to wring the last bit of usefulness out of me. Collaboration with singer/songwriter Paul Field and evangelist Rob Frost led to a hugely successful show based on the Lord's Prayer, which in turn led to the number-one hit single *Millennium Prayer* for Cliff Richard.

By the year 2000 complications arising from the dystrophy meant months in hospital, many of them in intensive care. And yet as I lay unable to even breathe for myself, at a point of utter weakness and hopelessness, I was also entering into the most fulfilling part of my life. In March of that year my son was born, mercifully free of the genetic condition that has in many ways shaped my life. And as I slowly regained much of my strength and returned to working (albeit with great difficulty) I have watched and delighted in his progress from being as helpless as I was around the time of his birth to being a vibrant, creative being. A few years later his brother was born, also free of the muscular dystrophy. As I write this, he lies asleep next to me, exhausted from a morning at nursery.

Bobby Ball

Bobby Ball has been in show business for forty-two years, and appeared in the fifth series of I'm a Celebrity . . . Get Me Out of Here! *In 1984 he became a Christian and he now spends four months a year preaching the word of God around the country. Bobby lives in Lancashire with his wife Von. He has three children and nine grandchildren.*

A long time ago a simple man came into being: he lived for thirty-three years and died a horrendous death because of his love for you and I. His name was Jesus Christ. He gave us hope in the fact that for all our terrible sins that we have committed, we could have an abundant life that would last for an eternity. He accomplished this by his death. He could promise these things because he was God incarnate. He was God who came to earth as Jesus Christ. He was all things to all men.

But my reason for hope is not that I will be forgiven or that I will live with Jesus. **That's a fact**. Why? Because Jesus says so. My reason for hope is that people who do not know him will find the true way to God through Jesus Christ. The world can be saved through him.

Fiona Castle

Fiona is a speaker and author. She is actively involved in the Roy Castle Lung Cancer Foundation, which her husband set up shortly before his death. Fiona was a key figure in campaigning for the British smoking ban that came into effect during 2007.

Like any youngster, I had hopes and dreams of how my life would pan out. I loved to dance and sing, and with considerable self-sacrifice, my parents enabled me to go to a boarding school at the age of nine to train in ballet and theatre arts. Although I didn't achieve my ambition of becoming a ballerina, I enjoyed several years fulfilling my love of dancing and singing in shows, pantomimes and musicals. My direction changed when I met Roy, my husband-to-be. I chose to become a full-time 'housewife' and eventually a mother of four children. Again, I was filled with hope that all my dreams would come true and that life would be wonderful.

Reality set in, however, and after twelve years of intermittent struggles with depression and a seemingly unconquerable sense of failure, all hope had gone and I realized that something had to be done if I was to survive to care for my husband and children.

It was this recognition which led me to the eternal hope, which remains with me to this day.

In the quiet of my bedroom, I confessed to God that I could no longer cope. I cried out to him to do something if he was there and if he could hear me. He could and he did, because immediately the phone rang. The caller was a woman I had met a few times, but was not someone I would have expected to phone me socially. I knew her to be a Christian.

She said, 'Fiona, I don't know why I'm phoning you, but I've had you on my mind recently and have had this sudden urge to phone you. I feel as if you need to talk. Would you like to come over to my house for a chat?'

I was out of the house like a shot and poured out my problems to this lovely lady. She was a good listener.

Eventually she challenged me by asking if I had ever invited Jesus into my life. When I said 'No', she said, 'Well, don't you think it's about time you did?' 'Yes' was my timid and fearful answer. She prayed with me and helped me to understand the significance of taking that step. It was the best decision of my life. I experienced the most amazing peace I had ever known. That peace has never left me because it was not related to my circumstances. God didn't change those, but he did change my attitude.

From that moment, my hope was not in the success I could be as a person, as a mother or as a wife, but rather in the hope that I have through the death and resurrection of the Lord Jesus, who died in my place for the mess I had made of my life. I was forgiven and could start afresh. I knew, and still know, that I am loved, even though I fail many times.

My self-esteem is not dependent on others. My peace is in being where God wants me to be and doing what God wants me to do.

My hope of eternal life was affirmed through the wonderful visions of heaven Roy experienced shortly before he died. He became not only peaceful about dying, but excited, as the Lord prepared him for what was ahead.

Life isn't easy, but then Jesus never said it would be, but he did tell us to be of good courage, because he has overcome the world and through him, we too have his strength to overcome.

Tom Lister

Tom is a professional actor, currently appearing in Emmerdale. *Tom has also worked on* Heartbeat. *He lives with his wife and son in the heart of North Yorkshire.*

It is a privilege to be asked to contribute to this book, for I believe that God calls us to tell our story. We have no idea of the power and the potential that our experience of faith has to affect others. What may seem to us like a small insignificant detail in our own lives, could be the major factor in leading someone else to God. So here's my story.

I grew up in a tiny village in the Yorkshire Dales. I went to church from an early age, spending time in Sunday school and youth groups. I was lucky to have a great group of friends around me, many of whom I am still close to today.

I actually made a commitment to follow Jesus when I was nine years old. I don't remember much about it – there was a lady preaching at church and she asked if anyone would like to make a decision to accept Jesus as their Saviour and enter a relationship with him. I felt like she was talking directly to me and I remember nervously raising my hand. She prayed for me and that was that. I made the same response at the end of a few more services until my Mum told me, 'It's OK, you only need to do it once!' So that was it, I was a Christian. I wish I could say everything made sense from that point onwards, or that my life was plain sailing, but unfortunately that wasn't the case.

By the time I reached eighteen, I had done quite well at school, got good grades and was considering university. Yet while I was studying for my A levels I started to get a passion for acting. After appearing in a couple of school shows and studying English Literature, my original plan to become a PE and Geography teacher faded rapidly and I decided to defer my university place.

On finishing school, I joined a Christian theatre company for two years. We toured the UK performing a play and sharing our faith in schools and youth groups. This gave me the confidence to have a crack at getting into drama college. I auditioned for a couple of schools and was accepted into Birmingham School of Acting. After a three-year course, which I thoroughly loved, I graduated, got an agent and now (drum roll, please) am a professional actor.

It was five years between the point when I left high school and graduated from college. Whilst that time was an amazing, exciting journey on which I firmly believe God directed me, the choices I made meant my faith took a pretty major battering during this period.

When I was eighteen years old, I went on holiday to Greece with some of my friends. This was the first real holiday we had all been on together, and as I'm sure you can imagine, we let our hair down. I lost my virginity and this totally rocked my world. Having grown up in church and been taught to believe that sex was to be kept between a husband and a wife, I felt an immense sense of guilt and shame about what I had done.

I came home from that time away and told a couple of people in my church what had happened. They prayed with me and I said sorry to God for what I had done and that was it, or so I thought. What actually happened was that sex became a real area of temptation in my life. I struggled with this problem throughout the time I spent in the theatre company and in drama college.

After spending three years in Birmingham, I reached the end of my studies and I felt that my life was at a major crossroads. I was about to graduate and had two options:

1: Go to London. This was what everyone was advising me to do if I wanted to 'make it in the business'.

2: Move back home and try to get my life back together.

I chose to move back home to Yorkshire and I can safely say that it was one of the most significant decisions I have ever made. I needed to find a way to get back to being true to myself and had I gone to London, I can honestly say I am not sure what would have happened to me. I was in a place where I seemed to be living desperately trying to please everyone else but me. I was involved in many different friendship groups and was a different person in each group, depending on who I thought they wanted me to be. At the end of my time in Birmingham I decided enough was enough.

I managed to break my destructive cycle of behaviour, but it wasn't easy. I spent one evening being prayed for by a few people from the local church and I told them everything I had done over the past five to six years. I bared my soul that night; all the ugliness that I had tried to keep covered up was brought out into the open. As I shared what had happened, I began to feel a freedom that I hadn't experienced before. I really believed that God had forgiven me and that I didn't need to beat myself up with guilt and shame. I realized that God didn't want me to feel like that. He wanted me to know that Jesus died to pay for *all* of the rubbish stuff that I had done in my life. He died to set me free to live the life that I was created to live. I started to really understand what the word 'grace' means; that it is the power to change, it is getting what we don't deserve. It is Jesus dying on the cross to bridge the gap between God, who is perfect, and we, who are imperfect.

I was freed then and life since then has been a different experience. It has not been easy, by any means, but I have a new-found strength that I never had before. I have had to become wise. I have strong friends around me who keep me accountable and honest.

I don't for a minute think God let me go through years of screwing my life up in order to teach me a lesson. We all have choices; we often make the wrong ones and have to live with the consequences. Yet God is able to rescue us from any situation. He can bring great things out of what seem to be the most hopeless of circumstances.

I am now married to the most beautiful girl I have ever met and we have a little one-year-old boy together. I thank God so much for helping me turn my life around. If my story can help someone find hope in the midst of their circumstances then it has definitely been worth sharing.

My reason for hope is found in these lyrics

> Not because of who I am,
> But because of what You've done.
> Not because of what I've done,
> But because of who You are.
> > From *Who am I?*, Casting Crowns

Five

Business and Organizations

Mike Ochsner

Mike Ochsner is the former Controller of the world-famous brands Billabong USA and Hurley International. He is also one of the leaders of Christian Surfers USA.

I am living the dream: as a retired surf industry executive I live in sunny Florida, surfing daily as the conditions allow, spending time with my children and grandchildren and staying in touch with many friends back in southern California. But this wasn't my dream. I never thought about early retirement, living on an island in Florida, or certainly not earning that retirement through surfing. When I took up the sport at the age of twelve, there was no 'surf industry', and my dream was to be an engineer with surfing as only an enjoyable pastime. My life's journey is evidence of the existence of God and that he is the only true reason for hope.

Thirty years ago it may have seemed that I was living the American dream. I married Sandi, my high school sweetheart while in college, had two daughters, bought a house and had a decent job working for a defence contractor. We lived in Huntington Beach, California, and that afforded me the opportunity to surf regularly. However, after returning from a two-week vacation in Hawaii I realized that something was missing. I wasn't content and I was without hope.

It was then that I decided that my happiness would be found aboard the Nalu II, a 47-foot sailboat that I found for sale in Dana Point Harbor. A former Trans-Pac winner, she had eleven bags of sails. What better escape than to sail off into the South Pacific in search of adventure and surf? Since we had recently sold our house and were renting while our new one was being built, it would be an easy matter to pull the plug on the house and buy the boat. So I put $1000 down and started planning.

I should mention that at this point in our marriage, my bride and my girls had accepted Jesus as their personal Saviour, but I was going it alone. It is interesting how God works in our lives, even when we aren't aware of him. Their salvation was the result of my taking a class in World Religion while in college and that awakening my wife's interest in her Lutheran roots, which culminated in all my girls accepting Jesus as Lord.

I thought that I had everything covered – we could pay cash for the boat and live aboard while we familiarized ourselves with sailing – and my cousin could join us to help sail the boat while his wife tutored our children. I figured that we could survive a few years and then either I would get a job in Australia or we would come back to the US and start over.

While all this was in motion, my wife had a vision of me standing on the deck of Nalu II, with my hands upraised, giving praise to God. Meanwhile, as the point of decision drew near, I had an overwhelming sense of selfishness for unilaterally deciding the future of our family. On my way home from work one afternoon, I stopped by the house under construction to see how it was progressing. I was there, strolling about, thinking how our lives were going to radically change, and I realized that I was indeed selfish and that I should not go through with this ridiculous plan. I drove home and told Sandi that I was going to cancel the deal for the boat and we would continue to live on solid ground. Since she was in fact a non-swimmer it is needless to say that she was elated.

My wife and children may have been happy, but what about me? Although I felt good that I had made a self-less decision, I was still lost, looking for satisfaction in the wrong places. It was then that God intervened again, and while sailing with my cousin on our catamaran, my lung collapsed. Since it had happened to me once before during my drag racing days, I knew what had happened and went to the doctor who confirmed my diagnosis and admitted me to hospital. My wife asked if someone at the church could come and pray for me, but not wanting to be a hypocrite, I said no. Imagine my surprise when a long-haired, bearded guy came into my room with a Bible in his hand saying that he was from Calvary Chapel and was here to pray. It turned out that my oldest daughter had told her teacher about my hospitalization and he sent the pastor. During his visit he confronted me with the gospel of Jesus Christ and challenged me to try him for two weeks to find out if he does truly change lives and give peace. What could I do? If I was truly open-minded, then I had to accept the challenge. Otherwise, I was just making excuses. So I prayed to ask Jesus to come into my life on a 'trial basis'. The change was immediately apparent to me. I was no longer relying upon my own meagre talents and abilities, but rather upon the Creator of the universe.

I started reading the Bible, attending church, and praying, asking him to complete the work that he wanted to do in my life. At the end of the 'trial' I was convinced that he was real and that I couldn't live without him and so I prayed to make it permanent. Life didn't get noticeably easier, but living did. I found that my outlook changed both at home and in the office; I received several promotions at work and was enjoying learning about God through church and personal study. And it was through my pastor that I met Bob

Hurley. Bob was at the time a well-regarded surfboard shaper.

I was looking to buy a new surfboard and knew of Bob so I went to the local glass shop where he shaped and ordered a 6'4" squash-tailed thruster. It was the best board that I had ever ridden to date and I became friends with Bob. Shortly afterward, he told me that he was going to open a surf shop, and, since I was an accountant, I offered my services to him as a friend. My desire was to help a friend in Christ and nothing else. However, it turned out to be a good deal for both of us, since he generously gave me surfboards in exchange for my services. It was from the Hurley Surfboards shop in Costa Mesa, California that Billabong USA was birthed and my official entrance into the 'surf industry' was made. As Billabong grew, it was clear to me that God had arranged this relationship and that he was providing the means for me to exit the 'bomb business' and enter into the 'surf business'. I quit my job at Hughes Aircraft and became the full-time Controller for Billabong USA.

And the rest is history. Billabong USA flourished and eventually gave way to the founding of Hurley International. This was subsequently purchased by Nike. After a few years at the 'new' Hurley, it was time for me to move on so I took my leave to contemplate what the next phase of life would look like. Since then I have found satisfaction serving at Calvary Chapel Vero Beach, as a member of the Board of Directors of Christian Surfers USA, and doing some business consultancy.

The Bible states that we should 'always be prepared to give an answer to everyone who asks you to give the reason for the hope that you have' (1 Pet. 3:15) and so I have written this brief autobiography as a way to inform you, the reader, of my experience of trusting in God and my reason for hope. God has proved himself over and over to me and I believe that he will to you as well.

Alison Hopkinson

Formerly the Financial Director of Dell Computers for various European divisions, Alison Hopkinson is now a freelance Finance Director working for small growing companies. She is married and has two teenagers and two Labradors.

Back in my cash-strapped student days I landed a job as a waitress by giving my word that I'd work through the whole of the season, yet knowing full well that after a few short weeks I'd take the money and run off to enjoy the rest of the summer. I was amazed at how sympathetic and understanding the manager was as she swallowed my story that I had to hurry home to my cancer-stricken mother. A short while later, Dad came to take me home, unaware of my subterfuge and accompanied, to my surprise, by my fit and healthy mum who insisted we all enjoyed a hearty meal in the restaurant before returning home! She was as bemused as I was embarrassed, as my manager came to our table and gave Mum a massive hug and asked how she was coping, how the treatment was going and how she was managing to stay so positive. I sat there wanting to die, for the ground to open up and swallow me. Why had I told such an awful lie? That day I vowed never to lie again.

Ten years later, one beautiful summer's day, I stood in a little village church surrounded by my family and friends, with Katie, my three-month-old daughter in my arms. I felt so happy. We had wanted a baby for a long time and now at last here she was being christened. I was so proud to be showing her off to the people who meant the most to me in the world. It was one of the happiest moments of my life and a time to reflect upon just how much I had: I was deeply in love with my husband, had a successful career and now a lovely little girl. At that moment life could not have been more perfect until, to my shame, I heard myself lying again as, in front of all those witnesses, I promised that I'd bring my daughter up in the Christian faith. I remembered my personal vow about not lying and was deeply upset. How could I lie so publicly? I was horribly ashamed of myself and it was a feeling that just wouldn't go away.

At this time I was running the UK finance team for Dell Computers, managing around thirty staff. I was driven, results-focused, hard-working and rapidly rising through the ranks and I expected the same attitude from my staff. Part of the staff management process was to submit to what was known as a 360 Degree Personal Assessment. My bosses, peers and staff were all asked to rate me on my management style and effectiveness. The results overwhelmingly showed that people saw me as a hard-nosed, heartless bitch. I was sure that wasn't the real me, but knew that as a woman in a man's world to show emotions would be seen as weakness. Never-the-less I was deeply upset by my character assessment.

Soon afterwards a new sales director joined us at Dell. His style of management interested me. He seemed to genuinely care about his staff and treat them as people with lives that had value and dimension outside of the company. This was new and intriguing. Here was someone who was successful in his career and was, I discovered, openly passionate about God. That passion was contagious and after a long journey of exploration that took me from fusty to buzzing churches and into relationships with Christians who understood where I was coming from and where I needed to be, I finally gave my life to the Lord. I am now passionately in love with God and know he is passionately in love with me, warts and all, as I constantly struggle to keep him at the forefront of my life. I'm a strong individual who has achieved significant success through sheer will-power and brute force and I frequently have to remind myself that letting Jesus lead the way is not a sign of weakness. 365 days after becoming a Christian I had another 360 Degree Assessment at work and was struck to hear that the views of my manager, peers and staff had completely changed: I was now regarded a great person to work with. Furthermore, a month later, the 'new me' was promoted to the challenging role of Financial Director of Dell France.

God didn't just want to transform me, he wants to transform the people around me and I believe that he will use me to bring others to know him. I love helping people on their own journey of discovery, especially through the Alpha course. However my deepest hopes and prayers are for my two beloved teenagers to lead happy and fulfilled lives. That hope lies in the grace of an amazing Father who, when seeing me standing in his house offering up empty vows, drew closer and closer until I could finally grasp his transforming love and allow it to flow into my life and through my family. He is amazing, I promise.

Greg Valerio

Greg Valerio is a social entrepreneur and has been called many things: maverick, passionate, emotional, rebel, scruffy and visionary. He is the founder of Cred Jewellery, the UK's first ethical jewellery company and works directly with community groups in India, Colombia, Ethiopia and Nepal.

I am a committed advocate for the poor and the marginalized. If you are poor, hope is the one thing that is denied you. That day-to-day existence, a life without horizons, robs you of a future, and slowly your humanity shuts down: horror becomes your inheritance.

Like most people, I had an intellectual understanding that God cares for 'the poor', but it wasn't until I visited Ethiopia shortly after becoming a Christian that I had a life-changing Christ encounter, meeting the people behind that label. 'Justice for the Poor' was no longer a worthy add-on to Christian faith, but a central tenet, a revolutionary call to arms, and a revelation. I realized that Jesus Christ was poor. God started at the bottom of the pile and offered the tangible hope of freedom and liberation to those whose future hope was being robbed daily. And I realized that anyone who chose to follow him had to follow in his footsteps.

This is why I established Cred Jewellery, an ethical business that seeks to redefine how international trade should work. It might seem a big leap from the slums of Ethiopia to the glitzy world of gold and diamonds, but it has been a journey following God's imperative to pursue justice and transformation.

I started by setting up the charitable Cred Foundation to deliver development education in schools, and to support innovative international projects bringing God's transformation to some of the poorest places on earth. However, it soon became clear that international trade, currently a means of institutional oppression, could be the very means of transformation in the future. I realized that this was more likely to take place by 'sitting at the table' of business rather than raging against the machine from the outside. It seemed better to model an alternative from the inside.

Cred Jewellery was built on that basis. Since Fair Trade is currently the best way to guarantee a fair deal for the poorest people, we're delivering Fair Trade gold, platinum and silver with certified environmental sustainability, and hope to deliver diamonds in due course. The mining sector is a good place to start: If we can make it work in an industry known for the most appalling social and environmental exploitation, there's no reason why it can't work elsewhere. It is also a sweet irony that the very economic system currently working against the poor, the materialistic consumer-focused system of which we are all a part, and of which jewellery is emblematic, is now working to alleviate their suffering.

So why do I have hope? Because I'm not the only one who thinks this way. There are many within the church of Jesus Christ who feel the same sense of sorrow and indignation, and who are looking to be the change they want to see in the world, as Gandhi once said. There are also many in the business community who resonate with these values, but who just haven't had an alternative to work with so far.

And what do I hope for? That the church would embrace the call to outwork transformation in the world and do as Jesus did: pull down the walls that exclude the marginalized and redistribute its wealth to the poor.

Jim Moriarty

Jim Moriarty, CEO of Surfrider Foundation, is an avid surfer, entrepreneur and innovator. He lives with his wife and two children in California, where he also mentors high school students.

> The disciples went and woke him, saying, "Master, Master, we're going to drown!" He got up and rebuked the wind and the raging waters; the storm subsided, and all was calm. "Where is your faith?" he asked his disciples.
>
> In fear and amazement they asked one another, "Who is this? He commands even the winds and the water, and they obey him." (Lk. 8:24,25)

I sit here writing this column in San Diego in October 2007. It is day five of a set of fires that have forced over five hundred thousand people to flee from their homes. The headlines are: 'Southern California on fire'.

We were evacuated a few days ago. My daughter quietly walked out to the car with her single bag saying, 'I have a few T-shirts, some shorts and my Bible.' I was proud of my family's courage.

We fled north, away from the fires and smoke. We prayed the simple prayer 'God, your will be done.' We, as a family, acknowledged that God was in control of nature and not us.

The fires got closer and closer to our home and we were beginning to think we could lose everything. We added to our prayers, asking for as many lives to be saved as possible and for the winds, fuelling the fires with great intensity, to die down. We remembered the verses above: God is in control.

We woke up the next day and before we checked the news we prayed again. The various reports said the winds had decreased from 35 mph to . . . zero. No wind. I cannot capture in words the feeling I experienced at that moment. The closest I can come is to say I felt God. I was reminded of God's divine power on our earth.

Working for Surfrider Foundation, I know that God is in control. It's an organization oriented around the preservation of our oceans, waves and beaches. We work hard, day in and day out, to conserve what we love. Humans may be messing things up constantly but we'll try to reverse those mistakes.

My hope is we not only find joy in our oceans, waves and beaches – my hope is we understand our responsibility to look after our natural surroundings. My hope is we acknowledge God as the master architect of all these things and praise him for what he's entrusted to us.

My hope is that we can ignore all the chatter around us every day and see God.

Greg Hawkins

Greg Hawkins is formerly the CEO of BUY.com and is part-owner of Covered Images, a digital photography company. He has been involved in publishing a surfers' Bible. Greg is semi-retired and lives with his wife and son in San Clemente, California.

I was brought up in a Christian home and experienced the love of Christ from my parents each day of my youth. Unfortunately for much of my adult life I actually didn't place my hope in Christ but myself. How many believers, if being honest, would say the same? How many of us sit in churches on Sunday, but come Monday we rely on ourselves for our everyday life?

I had a selfish perspective that drove me to desire success and personal fulfillment. I submitted very little in my day-to-day life and allowed little room for any relationship with God. As I experienced more success, I found that I was the one designing life and the rules by which I was going to live.

My career choices had led me to the technology sector during the 1990s, a period of incredible growth. The success that came during this period provided me with more reasons to rely on myself. This success took a toll on my marriage. Who had time for a real relationship? What applied to God also applied to my wife. I was busy climbing the ladder and enjoying the fruits of my success. This is common behaviour in successful men; as a result, sometimes we need 'our' dreams to come crashing down around us for us to realize that we need God's grace and that he alone can provide us with true hope.

This turning point for me began in early 1999. I became the CEO for a high-profile internet company. The day the company went public, my stock options were worth over $100 million. Before I could cash them in, the internet bubble burst and over the next nine months my stock became worthless. This led me to the final catalyst for change. I still had enough money to retire. My plan was to surf and play golf. Shortly after my decision, I had corrective eye surgery which failed. I ended up with double vision. 'My' plans were really messed up.

I finally got to the point that I realized I could not make it happen. The death of all my dreams, as shallow as they were, got me to a place where I finally reached the end of 'myself'. I finally became a candidate for grace, God's unmerited favour. It was almost a 'death experience' that had to take effect for me to begin to grow.

I am happy to say the past years have produced a new plan: one that has made me hungry to grow in the knowledge of God's will for my life. I have reversed the order: I no longer want independence and to make my own rules. My relationships with my wife, family and others are based more on serving than receiving. My hope lies solely in the knowledge that for life to work I need to 'seek first the kingdom of God' and in fact all the things of life will be 'added unto me'. (Mt. 6:33, NKJV)

Paul Williams

Paul Williams is an entrepreneur and the CEO of MLS Group Plc which runs MLS business centres, the second largest serviced office business in the UK. The group also run similar businesses in Asia and South America. Paul is married with two children and lives in Surrey. He took part in the TV programme Secret Millionaire.

As a businessman and entrepreneur I am an optimist and it is part of my job to give people inspiration and hope – to inspire and envision the teams that work for me to believe in themselves – and through doing that overcome obstacles and make things happen.

Deep down somewhere inside I know that my personal hope is based on relationships, firstly and most importantly my friendship with Jesus Christ and then with my wife, children, extended family and a handful of real friends.

The challenge however is that day-to-day in the business world I am persuaded to believe and promote the notion that hope is based on what I achieve and on what I am able to earn and buy. It is so easy to think that if only I was a little bit more successful that I would reach nirvana, be at peace, have a deeper joy and be more secure.

However, I remember the time around twenty years ago when in despair, feeling desperately alone, I faced potential bankruptcy and possibly even an unjustified jail sentence. A close, real friend, not a 'pretend' friend as

I call them, came around to see me, put his arm around my shoulder, confirmed his commitment to me whatever happened and then prayed God's peace into my life. I realized again that only God can offer real security. It is only by prioritizing the relationships that matter to me, those whom I love and love me that I will find real joy and security.

Building a multi-national company means I travel extensively and regularly meet the rich and famous whose lifestyles many covet. They often seem to be lonely: their wealth makes it hard for them to trust others and they question the motives of those around them, even their close family. I am discovering that it is more often in those whom I meet through my charitable activities who serve and live simply – like some of my friends in India and in the mountains of Nepal – that one finds a deep unshakeable hope based in God.

I recently spent several days in a remote village with no phone or email access. Sitting on a dirt floor in a mud hut one evening, eating the chicken that had been killed in my honour, I watched the sun set over the mountains with some new friends. All the 'stuff' that promises security and hope was not available to them but their contentment, peace and deep faith in God was profoundly moving and challenging. I still have so much to learn from them.

Six

Sport

Six

Sport

Chris Lenton

Chris Lenton is a former first-class rugby player with Wasps FC and National and World Masters Gold medal winner as an oarsman. He still competes in National and World Masters events. Chris is currently a director of the Institute of Chartered Secretaries and Administrators. He is married to Sally and has two teenage daughters.

I have been a Christian most of my life and much of my life as a child was centred around St Michael's and All Angels Church in west London where we lived. I sang in the choir, attended the church cubs and scouts and my father nearly became ordained in the 1960s. During this time I was a Christian with a small 'c' as it were; in that I was going through the motions and keeping up attendances but not really embracing the life as outlined by Jesus. I did conduct my life on the basis of Christian values and I have my parents to thank for that.

I have had an extraordinary sporting career in rugby and rowing. God has blessed me with strength, particularly an incredibly strong back. Through the 1970s I won national titles at rowing and played first-class rugby. However it was not until 1984 when I met my wife that I started to embrace the Christian faith with any degree of zeal. I attended a meeting in Marlow where the speaker gave a Christian perspective on marriage. For the first time someone was making the gospels relevant to me and to twentieth-century living: it was as if the speaker was talking directly to me. I wanted to hear more and

attended the King's Church in Marlow shortly before it
merged with River Church. They met on Sunday morning, which was a bit tricky as I was rowing. However, I
persuaded the other rowers to go out earlier so that I
could get to church on time. In fact, over the months as
we were preparing for Henley Royal Regatta, they
became more concerned about getting me back on time
than I did. From this time on I became a Christian with
a big 'C'.

I am an optimist and an encourager and see immense
positive reasons for hope in Jesus. The work of our
church over the last twenty-three years has quite literally
changed lives for the better not just here in our local community but internationally. The teaching and support
others and I have received over this period has reinforced
my values and equipped me to deal with a whole range
of issues. I see the Evangelical Alliance growing and new
churches springing up all over the place. This gives me
enormous hope. The way in which the message is presented is critical, as the established church is finding out.
I have a background in marketing and we have to change
how we present the gospel to the different market seg-
ments. My parents, bless them, are eighty-three years old
and they enjoy a traditional service; however their
granddaughters can't cope with it and prefer a more
modern version, tailored to their needs.

I have occupied a number of senior posts in my professional career and this has presented several ethical
dilemmas. In this I am supported by the River Business
Group who offer advice and give prayer support. My
faith has carried me through many difficulties and I
have had countless answers to prayer. I try to be an
example in the workplace and incredibly many people
have been touched by it. Being a Christian is the hardest
thing I have done, but I do see my colleagues enquiring

and seeking a spiritual dimension to their lives. I see an improved value system pervading communities. I see wrecked lives redeemed.

The new challenges will be to take on the new forces of secularism, paganism and the competing faiths that pervade this country. Many people are agnostics but the question is still asked 'Is this it . . . is this all there is to life?' I don't think so and I will continue to speak to people about hope in the resurrection and operate as a Christian (with a big 'C').

Pete McKnight

Pete McKnight works full-time for the English Institute of Sport. He is a Strength and Conditioning Coach for the Olympic athletes based in the North. Pete is involved in leadership in his church and also works as a mobilizer for international mission, regularly helping facilitate the Kairos world mission course. He lives in Loughbrough with his wife and son.

As I was lying there, a hand stretched down towards me to pull me from my bed. I reached up and grabbed the hand and it gripped me firmly. It began to pull me upwards, through the ceiling, up through the clouds, and towards the sky. I knew it was Jesus pulling me upwards and taking me home. Suddenly someone jumped up from the earth and grabbed onto my feet to try and stop me leaving this earth. Then another person jumped and grabbed me round the waist. Soon, one after the other, people were jumping up and grabbing me to try and pull me back. With all these people dangling from my waist and legs the hand that held me firmly slowly began to loosen its grip. Before I knew what to do, the hand had let go and we were all falling back down to earth where we landed in a big pile with a thud.

I woke up and realized it had been a dream. I was still lying in the hospital bed in Chiang Mai, Thailand, where I had been for the past two days. My body was wasting away. For the past two weeks I had been getting weaker and weaker, suffering from an extremely high temperature and aching all over. Finally I decided to go to hospital. My wife and I were staying with my parents who have been missionaries in Thailand for many years. The doctors didn't know what was wrong or why I had lost 10 kilos of body weight in ten days, and was getting progressively weaker. I had almost lost hope. How could a young, fit guy like me, a guy who had everything going for him, be reduced to a curled-up wreck in a hospital bed, with no control over his deteriorating condition? There was nothing I could do. I was totally at the mercy of the doctors . . . and God.

Within a couple of days I was out of hospital and beginning to feel better. My strength was already returning and I started to understand the dream. I had been dying from undiagnosed malaria. No one knew what was wrong with me. My family had e-mailed people all over the world asking for prayer for my healing. In my dream I was leaving this earth. Jesus was taking me home to be with him and as he pulled me upwards, I looked into his eyes. However people all over the world were praying for me to stay. The people jumping up and grabbing onto me in my dream represented the prayers of all those friends from my church back in England, and countless others round the globe who were interceding for me. Their prayers were pulling me back down to earth as the hand was pulling me up. The hand released me and the prayers were answered. Jesus didn't put up a struggle, he let go, he knew my time had not come to leave. Too many people were praying for me, so he let me stay.

When I woke up from the dream the doctors came into my hospital room and told me I had malaria. The news excited me. It was the only hope I had had in weeks. I knew it was fairly easy to treat malaria. The problem was that prior to this, no one knew what was wrong with me, so I was just getting worse. Now they knew, I was convinced I would get better. The dream gave me hope. I wasn't leaving yet. The doctor gave me the appropriate medication over the next two days and then sent me home to recover. I felt better straightaway but it took me three months to get my life back to normal and to return to full fitness. God had healed me because of the prayers of my friends and family. When I was at the point of despair, when all hope was lost, God gave me a dream that gave me hope.

Brett Davis

Brett Davis is the International Director of Christian Surfers, which he pioneered in Australia in 1977. He is married with three children, and lives south of Sydney in the seaside village of Coledale.

Growing up as an Australian surfer I placed my hope, pre-internet surf-forecasting days, in the synoptic chart where my mates and I poured over onion-shaped patterns, anticipating new swells. The excitement of a solid groundswell was accompanied with nervous paddle-outs, huge drops, the hero tuberide and the 'after glow' of stories, washed down with coke and the local bakery fare. It was also accompanied by a let down as the swell disappeared as soon as it had appeared, leaving us hoping for more. I found myself longing for something more substantial. Jesus was that 'more'.

After struggling with how I 'fitted' as a Christian and as a surfer I have become comfortable in the skin, and wetsuit, God made me. Now having been in full-time ministry with Christian Surfers for over twenty years, it isn't the surfing that gives me hope. It isn't the great, and not-so-great, people that give me hope. It isn't the ministry results, or lack of, at times, that give me hope. It isn't even myself and my learned skills and experiences that give me hope. What does give me hope is not the waves that God made, but the God who made the waves. This rock-solid assurance that God is faithful.

I love Psalm 93,

> The LORD reigns, he is robed in majesty;
> the LORD is robed in majesty
> and is armed with strength.
> The world is firmly established;
> it cannot be moved.
> Your throne was established long ago;
> you are from all eternity.
> The seas have lifted up, O LORD,
> the seas have lifted up their voice;
> the seas have lifted up their pounding waves.
> Mightier than the thunder of the great waters,
> mightier than the breakers of the sea—
> the LORD on high is mighty.
> Your statutes stand firm;
> holiness adorns your house
> for endless days, O LORD.

I appreciate the immense ocean waves pounding both shorelines as well as the surfers on them. But look at the words that describe the God who made these waves: 'firmly established', 'cannot be moved', 'from all eternity', 'stand firm', 'endless days'.

I have been tempted many times to give up hope. I have been failed by friends, events and, most of all, by myself. However, God is the sure foundation, the solid ground in the shifting sands of this world. I am convinced that what I entrust to him will be kept for all time and eternity, regardless of what plays out in the wind-tossed waves of this world.

Debra Searle MBE

Debra Searle is a professional adventurer. Her expeditions have included rowing solo across the Atlantic and sailing around Antarctica. She has also launched two companies, been a TV presenter and is a published author and popular corporate speaker. Debra's spirit of adventure gained her an MBE. She lives in Devon with her husband Tim, where they are active members of Mutley Baptist Church.

By twenty-five years of age I had completed many expeditions but the biggest challenge yet lay on the horizon. I had entered the Atlantic Rowing Race with my then-husband, Andrew. 36 double-handed teams entered but we were the only mixed-sex team in the race. I was a foot shorter than Andrew, who was a top British rower, and had not rowed prior to signing up, so if anyone wasn't going to make it three thousand miles in a plywood rowing boat it was the wife!

But on our first night out at sea we discovered that the opposite was in fact true. Having lost sight of every other boat and the lights on land it became apparent that Andrew had a crippling phobia of open ocean. His condition deteriorated rapidly and dramatically so we were left with no choice but to call for rescue.

I decided to go on alone.

The journey was supposed to take us six weeks. Alone, it took me three and a half months. I saw no one. I just rowed every day, two hours on, one hour off, around the clock, seeing nothing but sky, sea and all the creatures in it. That is how God first started to re-kindle my hope. He had me alone and he had a captive audience.

The beauty I witnessed was unlike anything I had seen before. The colours of the vast array of fish, whales and sharks that would circle under my boat were stunning. These creatures have a gracefulness that, when witnessed in the wild, is breathtakingly beautiful. Some days I was so overcome by the intensity of the beauty that I would cry.

I found myself, through tears of joy, saying 'thank you' out loud over and over again because I knew that such beauty could not be by chance. Somebody must have engineered it and it was totally clear to me for the first time ever that that somebody was God.

So I started talking to him and he spoke back through my feelings and the thoughts in my head. I had such a strong sense that I could put my hope in him and that he was going to get me across that ocean – which was a good thing as there were hurricane winds and thirty-foot waves on more than a few occasions.

I wondered if I would still feel the same on dry land. Would I still believe, hope, trust in the Creator God? Did he have anything to say about my life and my future?

Mid-Atlantic I came close to being run down by a supertanker. On the verge of giving up I spoke to my twin sister by satellite phone. 'You can't give up,' she said. 'I believe that you are going to be a presenter on Grandstand.' I was furious with her for saying something so crazy when minutes before I had nearly died. Grandstand is the biggest sports programme on the BBC so it was hardly likely that a novice presenter would walk straight into a role there. Plus, I had no desire to be a television presenter. But God had given her a prophecy for me. She just could not tell me that at the time because it would have freaked me out and I probably would have run a mile from Christianity.

It took me one hundred and eleven days to row the Atlantic single-handed. Three other men tried a solo attempt but none of them made it. Within five months of completing my Atlantic crossing I presented my first programme for Grandstand. It's amazing what God has in store for us once we take that leap of faith and put our hope in him entirely.

Greg Morgan

Greg Morgan is the Team Leader for the University Department at Christians in Sport. Its aim is to serve and support Christian sports-playing students to reach out to their club mates with the gospel. He is married and lives in Northamptonshire. Greg is a keen rugby player.

I had the privilege of being brought up in a sporty family. My father, a golf professional and a general sports enthusiast, fuelled a passion for sport in me from an early age. As I grew up it became a major part of my life whether it was cycling, playing rugby, golf or surfing. I continue to be passionately absorbed by any and every sport.

Growing up I dreamt of being the best I could possibly be, particularly at rugby: I hoped to one day play professionally and dreamt of representing my country. One season at school I broke my arm playing and was unable to train so I was sent to a classroom to read. The only book I could find was a small Bible (actually the New Testament and Psalms) which reluctantly I began to read. The book really irritated me, as the section I read spoke of this man Jesus: I'd heard of him but knew little about him. The things Jesus said and did and the claims he made seemed outrageous yet, if true, of massive importance. I became frustrated that everyone seemed to know who he was but no one had ever told me.

For the next six months I avidly tried to grasp his identity and what he had done; I attended church, which

I found weird yet intriguing, but it wasn't until I attended a weekend away, where young people from the church went to play sport with other churches, that I fully grasped who he was.

It was the Sunday morning just before we were to head into our final day of matches, and a guy from Birmingham got up and explained that my greatest need in the whole of my life was to have my sins forgiven . . . not to be the world's best sportsman. He went on to state that Jesus had come to earth, lived the perfect life and died the most hideous death on a cross . . . for me . . . to pay the price for my rebellion. But that wasn't it, the guy went on to explain that three days later he rose again, proving his power over death, proving that the penalty for my sin had been paid and that he offered me real life . . . true life with him, now and forever. Right there and then, faced with what he did, my heart broke and I put my hope in him.

Fifteen years on, I continue to be a passionate sports player. However my hope is no longer in my own strength and ability – but in the strength of the God who loves and laid down his life for me.

Richard Mulder

Richard Mulder was a professional skateboarder. He now uses this platform to speak of a life of purpose rooted in God. Richard has travelled to many countries sharing the Good News through skateboarding and preaching. He and his wife Sarah live in Newport Beach, California.

> As it was in the days of Noah, so it will be at the coming of the Son of Man. (Mt. 24:37)

You don't have to be a rocket scientist to look around the world you live in to come to the conclusion that there are serious issues on Planet Earth: war, famine, disease, hatred . . . and the list goes on. The drugs we take to make the problems and pain go away don't work either. They just make the dark hole in our hearts deeper. I clearly remember, before my eyes were opened by the reality of Jesus' love for me, I would smoke weed and instead of getting high I would get fearful and anxious as I thought about all the problems we face. I was over-whelmed by torment and hopelessness.

I remember asking, 'Does anyone care? Does God care?' I believe those questions are placed in our hearts, just as God has put eternity in our hearts. He has planted a portion of eternity that makes us cry out for something eternal. That's why we can go anywhere in the world and find people hungry for meaning, participating in palm reading and fortune-telling. You can see our interest in ghosts and the afterlife reflected in books and TV shows.

What we're really looking for is hope. We are looking for a reason for existence.

I have found my hope in a daily encounter with Jesus Christ. The story of the bloody cross does not lie. God loves me with a jealous love. My hope is not in a theology, but in the reality of his being. The uncreated God bore all the junk of humanity in order to re-establish a relationship with us. When you realize how huge is the heart of God and how much he is interested in every detail of your life, you really begin to live the way he intended. At that place, nothing can outshine the reality of the hope he alone brings.

The Bible is full of scriptures that speak about the generation on the earth at the time of his coming. The time of Noah was similar to our own. Evil was rampant on the earth but there was a man named Noah who walked with God and shared his hope. God took him and all who discerned his voice into the ark of his safety. This is my reason for hope.

No matter what evils go on, God's love, demonstrated on the cross, is still speaking and beckoning a generation to him. This love is the driving force that anchors me. I can see him in everything, working for his reward and inheritance: you and I. Like Noah's ark, my only hope is to be led, captivated, and abandoned to the Father's love.

Seven

Musicians and Worship Leaders

Ben Cantelon

Ben Cantelon is a Canadian-born worship director for Soul Survivor Church in Watford, pastored by Mike Pilavachi. He is also one of the worship leaders at the Soul Survivor conference.

I always had a desire to someday live in the UK but had no idea how that would happen. I'm originally from a little town in Canada called Langley but I have been living in the UK for about four years now. It was a far-fetched idea and I thought it would never happen. The reason why I was drawn to the UK was worship. When I was a teenager I had the worship CDs of Matt Redman, Delirious?, Tim Hughes and others. I listened to these albums and I was amazed at the heart behind the songs, they were intimate, desperate and real. I could believe what they were saying and I couldn't help but worship. It's strange but even as a teenager I felt there was a connection to these songs, as if I knew these people. At the age of sixteen I heard about this church called Soul Survivor in a place called Watford. I was so desperate that I even started looking at universities in that area just so that I could go to this church to understand more of the heart of worship. But I thought it was just a dream.

I carried on living my life unsure of what God had in store for me. I knew I was called to worship but to what extent I had no idea. I had never led worship, I had never written a song. I was just a musician. A few years later I got a phone call and was asked to play at a youth conference where Tim Hughes was leading and Mike Pilavachi was speaking. I didn't even know who Mike Pilavachi was, but I thought I would take the opportunity. By this time I had forgotten about my dreams and was happy with where I was and what I was doing – but God had something different in store. When the conference was over, Mike and Tim sat me down and said 'We have loved getting to know you and were wondering if you would like to come to the UK to play at our youth festival, Soul Survivor?' I was completely shocked. I did not expect that at all. I really didn't know what Soul Survivor was until I came that summer in 2003, then I really knew who Mike Pilavachi was! I got to see Soul Survivor church in Watford, which I always wanted to do, and also see thousands of young people worshipping our God at the festivals. God challenged me while I was there. He was showing me and teaching me what worship really was about: it was an fantastic experience.

After that summer, I went back to Langley. I kept in touch with Mike and carried on with my life thinking that I had lived out a dream of mine: little did I know . . .

Soul Survivor asked me to join Mike and Tim at various events of theirs around the world, playing in the worship band. It was incredible to be able to travel and play music. Eventually I was invited to Watford to carry on working and travelling with Tim and to play with him. I couldn't believe it. God was opening doors of which I had never dreamed.

It was a difficult sacrifice leaving home and my family. It took me a long time to get over homesickness and to feel settled. However I think God honours those who step out and take risks. So I moved over in the summer of 2004 not knowing how long I would be here or where this crazy rollercoaster would take me. I enjoyed what I was doing and thought I was content. But again God had other things in mind. I came home from a trip one day and picked up an acoustic guitar in my bedroom and began to worship. As I sat there I felt God put a desire in my heart to lead worship, but I wasn't sure if it was just me or if it was actually God. So I left it with him and said 'If this is you, then you have to make this happen.'

Less than a week later, Mike phoned me and he said 'Mate, on my flight back from Australia, I felt God say that you are supposed to lead worship.' I couldn't believe it and was completely overwhelmed by God's faithfulness. I had led worship a few times back in Langley but it had never been my calling. I led worship for the first time in May 2005 and that summer, I led at the Soul Survivor festivals. After the festivals, Tim and Rachel Hughes left to work with our friends at Holy Trinity Brompton in London. Mike then asked me to be the Worship Director for the church.

So I had that dream. And just a few years later I find myself right in the middle of that dream. It is now my reality.

In sharing this with you, I hope it encourages you to keep going with the dreams that God has given you. He gives them for a reason and if you stay true to him and live out each day knowing that he is in control, you can watch him do things that you could never imagine.

Lindsay West

Lindsay West, aka Lindz West, heads up the Message Trust's flagship band, LZ7. Lindz was in the World Wide Message Tribe, and this is the next generation of the work to take the gospel relevantly and credibly to young people. LZ7 travels the globe, making God famous, profiling the Message Trust's schools' work and recruiting for their academy for creative evangelists. Lindz lives in Manchester with his wife Lucy.

Everyone buzzes about the word 'hope', even if you don't realize you do. For example, you know when you were a kid you used to have sleepless nights over what Santa was bringing you for Christmas . . . close your eyes and think about that feeling now . . . you hoped what you were getting was what you requested. You got excited about that hope because you knew that your mum and dad (Santa) were not going to let you down therefore you knew your hope had an outcome. Well . . . I know that the 'hope' I have in God has an outcome. If my mum and dad loved me so much to provide what I had hoped for, how much more will God come through for us with what we hope for? Without 'hope' we don't have anything to look forward to.

In Isaiah 40:31 it says 'but those who hope in the LORD will renew their strength. They will soar on wings like eagles; they will run and not grow weary, they will walk and not be faint.' How amazing is that? And that's just one promise about the hope that we have in God. So think about it. Where does your hope lie, do you have any hope? If not, check out the promises of hope in the Bible and you will be sure to 'renew your strength'.

David Hadden

David Hadden and his wife Ruth serve as part of the Ministry Team at Leicester Christian Fellowship, and are involved in leading the School of Worship. They have three children.

Since I became a Christian in the mid-seventies much has changed in society and in the church. My involvement has been with the training of worshippers, and that, too, has seen much change. And what about my hopes? These too have developed and changed.

My first taste of worship was in a small church filled with young people in the north-east of England. I was young at that time! I was a new Christian and wanting to learn about this new life upon which I had embarked. After a few years there, I moved to Bradford to attend Bible college. My life changed again as I was in the company of men and women who had given up many things to serve God. I was given responsibility to lead worship and direct the worship team at major Christian gatherings: Bible weeks in the Dales and Wales, organized by Covenant Ministries. We were riding a wave of faith and expectancy and yet there was still more to do. I was daring to hope I might become a well-known songwriter.

In Bradford I married my wife Ruth and we now have three children. After a decade there we moved to Leicester. A few years later we discovered Leicester Christian Fellowship. We were then fortunate to spend five years in the US, working in St Louis, Missouri. The pastor of the church in St Louis had been a fellow student at Bible college. God called us back across the Atlantic and we returned to Leicester. To our delight the church is now pastored by another college friend, Ian Rossol.

These last few years have been a steep learning curve and we now have even more hope in God than before. We have begun to see and experience his power and presence as we gather together as a fellowship. We all feel like we are learners all over again. Our faith, trust and passion are reaching a deeper level daily as we seek to divine God's will. Most of all, God longs for us to be in his presence. It is refreshing, yet challenging, to do that, as it makes everything else that is important fall into line behind the essential. We are seeking to speak God's words and make our actions one with his. Our lives are being enriched by meeting new people from all over the world, and we are discovering that God is speaking to them as he is to us.

My hope is that my life shows somewhat the life and passion of Jesus. My heart's cry is 'More, Lord'.

Myles Dhillon

Myles Dhillon is a music student at the London Guildhall and he is a rapper and all-round 'lyrical gangster'. He is currently working with LZ7.

Before I knew God my hope was purely in money. My family has a history in business. Growing up, I knew that to be successful I had to make money, one way or another. So, as a teenager I got into drugs, using and selling. I was good at it. Getting richer was my sole purpose; I even stopped using drugs after a while to focus more on dealing.

Also, I'm big into music. My hope was in my ability to rap and I felt most secure when beating others down lyrically in the playground.

As I grew older, a series of coincidences and God-encounters took place. There were also some admirable people in my life who became role models. This led me to leave that sheezey behind and follow God. It took some time for my knowledge of right and wrong to come into line; I was selling contraband cigarettes at a huge profit, while telling everyone I was saved. It was a journey for me, as opposed to an overnight transformation.

Today, my hope is in him. Without hope, or hope in him, life becomes pointless. I'm twenty-one years old now: I could focus the rest of my life on music, accumulating wealth, being the best rhymer and driving the illest car. All that stuff is OK but if you're doing it for the wrong reasons, it's not, it's a waste. You're going to die one day, maybe today, maybe tomorrow. And you'll take nothing to the grave with you.

I've lost my hope before, for real; it's not easy. I hate hypocrites, saying someone's bad when you're just as bad as them. In my late teens, I lost focus. I realized it's impossible to be perfect, and therefore I became a secret sinner. I still loved church but I didn't want to be like the hypocrites, so I dropped out. I lost hope in my Saviour. I have begun to realize now that I'm not the finished article; I'm still under construction.

I'm major focused on using what God has given me for his glory. I'm hopeful that God can use my skills as a platform for re-educating people about his real nature – and through that, I don't know how yet, generating wealth for his kingdom.

Andy Flannagan

Andy Flannagan spends his time gigging, cricketing, politicking and worship leading. He is on the leadership team of church.co.uk. Andy has written several books including God 360° *and* Distinctive Worship.

'Risk! That would be such a risk!'

Those were the words pounding through my head all through the festival. For the first time in my twenty-two years I was contemplating the possibility that I might not always be a doctor. Heresies don't come much bigger than that for a medical student.

Some clues had been divulged the preceding summer that this would be the case. I'd spent six weeks working and learning in one of the most disgusting places on earth. All of the refuse created by Cairo's twenty-eight million people ends up in a small area called Mokattam populated by twenty-eight thousand people and a similar number of animals. Right in the rotting midst of this sickly, sweet and overwhelming place was the hospital that became my temporary home. I was being exposed to the reality of people in desperate need, and growing in my soul was a passion to communicate about it, and other social inequalities for that matter. It was a summer when the volume knob was always at 'ten'. Compared to before, pain was deeper, joy was broader and moments became experiences.

So it was hardly a conscious decision to write songs. They had always been my exhaust pipe, after the combustion engine of heart and head had fired. I'd been given opportunities to spread this useful pollution to churches, events and bars. The songs seemed to challenge and bless, which was great, but surely it would always just be an entertaining sideline to having a 'proper job'. Fast forward to the Greenbelt festival at the end of that summer, performing for Tearfund.

I'd often wondered about the phrase 'in the groove'. Something useful is miraculously produced because this small needle fits perfectly into a slightly larger space. That was just a concept to me until I actually felt it happen; pouring my heart out in song, seeing a crowd connect with both words and melody, and feeling the very breath of my Creator down the back of my neck. I couldn't run from the question, 'Is this what I'm made for?'

That feeling however was rubbing up against a pretty harsh reality. The next two years of my life would consist of ninety-hour weeks, studying like I'd never studied before and being woken continually during the night by a bleeper that would have no regard for my beauty sleep. Where on earth could music and communication fit into that lifestyle? And would I not be in danger of throwing everything away on the strength of a gut feeling?

At the end of the festival, I sit on damp grass praying with ten thousand others. The word 'risk' is still stopping all other constructive thought like an M25 pile-up. A lady, whose quilted Scottish accent I will never forget, draws all our prayers to a close with these words, 'Lord God, may we be a people who take risks for you.' A bell clangs so loudly in my head that I presume everyone else is hearing the headlines too.

Risk?

I think I'll take it.

Steve Gambill

Former professional percussionist and now Rocknations Director and Youth Pastor at Abundant Life Church, Steve Gambill is passionate about helping people reach their God-given potential in life. He speaks to thousands every week through podcasting, FM radio, TV and outreach events. Steve is married to Charlotte and has two children.

My dreams started early in life. I wanted to be a famous musician. By the age of twelve I was practising drums for hours everyday. By the age of sixteen, I was playing and teaching professionally in the USA and had won a number of performance awards. Unfortunately, my identity had become tied up with how well I played and the acceptance I longed for proved to be short-lived. As long as the crowds cheered I was on a high, but when the applause stopped so did my happiness.

On the one hand you could look at my life and see a measure of success, but inside I was deeply unhappy. If I missed a few notes, I would sink into depression. So I redoubled my efforts and began to practise up to twelve hours a day. My parents were working long hours at their hotel restaurant, under tremendous financial pressure, which caused tension between my two sisters and myself. I tried to fill this depression and tension by partying with the 'in crowd', dating the prettiest girls and drinking. My life felt empty. Desperately, I searched for meaning in various world religions, philosophies and finally in drugs and alcohol.

Eventually things came to a crisis point following a televised performance at Seattle's Key Arena. Every time I picked up a pair of sticks the red light from the TV camera would light up. I thought this was my moment. But the next day I found out not one of my friends had seen the broadcast: I was gutted. Finally, I faced the fact that music would never take away the ache in my heart for love and acceptance.

Not knowing where to look, my partying took a vicious turn for the worse. Drunken excess brought on guilt, depression and loneliness. Many of my friends were becoming addicts and were offering me harder drugs than before. Despite the female attention I was receiving, I felt lonelier than ever. It wasn't long before my performance was affected and I was caught in a downward spiral. So I packed up my drums and drove thousands of miles to attend a music conservatory. It was then that God entered my life.

Jon Kasica is an amazing percussionist from the St Louis Symphony. At my first drum lesson with him, he asked me a question: 'Steve, do you want everything life has to offer?'

'Absolutely,' I replied.

'Then you need to be born again,' Jon said.

I had never heard that term before, but I had heard a little bit about God. When I was a baby I had cancer inside my nose and was treated at a hospital in Seattle. Radiation back then was experimental and 90 per cent of people treated developed secondary cancer from being over-radiated.

When my parents found out about these medical complications, they asked a Christian pastor to pray for my healing. Miraculously, the tumour vanished over the next few days. I had been completely healed and have been free of cancer ever since. I wondered, 'Could the

meaning I have searched so hard for be found in this
Jesus who healed me?' Could it be that simple?

Immediately after the lesson I went to my bedroom
and asked Jesus into my life. I felt a deep inner peace. I
got hold of a Bible and began to read it, trying to make
sense of the mess my life was in. By the end of the week
I had more questions than answers. I went back to my
next drum lesson thinking I would find out about being
born again, but before I could get the words out of my
mouth Jon asked me, 'Have you been baptized with the
Holy Spirit?'

I had never even heard of the Holy Spirit. I was still
trying to work out 'born again'. Jon opened his Bible to
Acts 19:2 and read, 'Did you receive the Holy Spirit
when you believed? No, we have not even heard that
there is a Holy Spirit.' I asked Jon to tell me more. So he
and his wife Paula prayed that the Holy Spirit would
baptize me and fill me with power. I had never felt anything like it. My desire for booze, partying, women and
worldly success instantly disappeared and an incredible
sense of love, acceptance and deep fulfilment replaced it.
I knew I had found what I was looking for. For the next
three days I felt a burning sensation throughout my
body; I was aware of the power of God for the first time.
I realized that God truly loves me and has a purpose for
my life.

Over the course of the next two weeks I told my
friends and colleagues about God. About twenty of
them also accepted Jesus and had similar encounters
with God. At the age of nineteen, I was happy for the
first time. I was so full of faith I felt as if I was bursting
at the seams with fresh hope for people. I realized that if
God could save me, then no one was too far gone for
God. Together with my new group of Christian friends
we started a band and I took every opportunity to share

my faith. Often on my walk to the St Louis Music Conservatory, I would tell people about Jesus and they would accept Jesus on the street.

Amazingly I began to have tremendous opportunities as a musician. Various entertainers and orchestras seemed to come and find me. I realized that God was opening doors I could never open and for almost a decade I played drums all over the world.

Then I had an opportunity to move to England. Weeks before I came, I met a beautiful Christian woman, Charlotte. Incredibly, Charlotte was from England and was about to move to the same city as me. We fell in love. We married in due course and now have two beautiful children.

In England, I started a youth conference and over the years have seen it grow to become a movement of young people and leaders in the thousands. We call it Rocknations. During that time, all kinds of miracles have happened: cancers have disappeared, relationships have been restored and hundreds have accepted Christ. And the best days for all of us are ahead.

Our hope, together with our team, is to see a generation rise up that will literally 'rocknations' for the glory of God. Will you join the cause?

Dave Bilbrough

With an appeal that spans all denominations, Dave Bilbrough's songs have become a staple part of church worship. They include 'All Hail the Lamb' and 'Abba Father'. He puts an emphasis on the grace and faithfulness of God, uninhibited praise and reconciliation.

It's not keeping up with the Joneses or discovering some secret new formula that gives me hope. Neither is it to be found in the trappings of a religious system, no matter how attractive it might appear, but my hope is found in the simple recognition that I am loved and accepted by God unconditionally and certainly undeservedly. So often we fall short of finding a real relationship with God because of our dependence on the outward to authenticate our faith rather than the inward discovery of his grace.

Walking in that grace has meant, for me, experiencing God's amazing provision in the face of circumstances that have screamed of anything but the goodness of God. He has spoken into my situations of need remarkably. Of course, there have been other times when the answers have not been forthcoming, but I'm thankful that he has brought the assurance of his presence. Looking back, this certainly achieved more than a temporary, quick-fix solution would have done.

As a writer of songs, returning to the stark truth that my approval in life is solely based on God's evaluation, not my own, often inspires a new song. That's my bedrock; that's where my inspiration flows from. A grace-based relationship offers endless possibilities for us to be creative in the way we live and the way we express our thanks to him. We can be free to be truly who God has made us to be instead of limiting ourselves by our own restrictions. We then become alive to the realm of possibilities that come from grace and faith.

Without grace, my life would be an endless treadmill of trying to do the right thing to please God. I still need reminding, and at times still look elsewhere for acceptance, but deep down I know it's God's grace that is my hope, sustenance and strength – and that grace is found in Christ who shines his light in my darkness and who is more committed to me than I will ever be to him. This is the reason for my hope.

Eight

Missionaries: At Home and Abroad

Joel Edwards

Joel Edwards is the General Director of the Evangelical Alliance UK and is a passionate advocate of both diversity and unity within the church. Joel also serves on a number of faith, government and public agency advisory groups and is a regular broadcaster in the UK and international media. He chairs the Micah Challenge International Council and is an honorary canon of St Paul's Cathedral.

I came to Britain as an eight year old in 1960. Even at that age I knew some 'facts' about the spiritual life of Britain. Britain, they said, was a spiritual graveyard where, on entry, Christian faith was suffocated by a godless society.

If you had told me then that Christians would march for Jesus through the streets of London in the 1970s I would not have believed you. And if someone had suggested that millions of people across the world would take part in Alpha suppers over the past ten years, carry out city-wide campaigns of mercy across the nation and have people praying 24/7 and gathering for Global Days of Prayer, it would have been incredulous. The Excel Centre on the Isle of Dogs in East London hosts up to 33,000 people who meet to pray all night, three times per year. It's a prayer meeting which stops the traffic.

Christians have also become more and more involved in the public square. Not long ago a Christian MP told me that he has never known as many Christians in the House of Commons as in the past five years. Christians are involved in campaigns against human trafficking, poverty and child pornography. International politicians are linking the prophetic name Micah (Micah Challenge) to the fight against global poverty. Christians are 'street pastors', they are 'Redeeming our Cities' and working against crime in 'Hope for London'.

Five years ago I sat with a group of Christian leaders to talk about a values campaign on hope. I was rather surprised that many of my colleagues felt that hope was somewhat esoteric; a vague Christian idea which couldn't possibly be translated into the cultural vernacular. So I am excited about 'Hope '08 – the whole Gospel for the whole nation for a whole year' and its ability to help people in Britain connect with the God of all hope.

I am hopeful because the hope, which a person has from coming to the cross of Christ and knowing the power of forgiven sins, is spilling into a world in need of practical love. And the hope within us which deals with the depravity of our sin is also helping people to understand that hope is also present in the gutters.

It's been some time since Britain could truly claim to be a Christian nation, and some churches still resemble the graveyards surrounding them, but there is an awful lot of God-inspired hope about.

Rich Wilson

Rich is the Team Leader of Fusion and works to see thousands of churches play their part in student mission. He is married to Ness and is involved in local church leadership.

The past is determined. Every thought, word and deed is cemented in history: collectively they create our present. The future, however, is open. Passions, creativity and hopes are all yet to be realized. This, for me, couldn't be more true than in the student world, where individuals' formal education is nearing its end and their lives are full of potential.

Today's students are often battered and bruised by the media caricatures of success and yet they believe strongly they can better themselves and the world. When fused with the call of God and the empowering of the Holy Spirit, young people are a force to be reckoned with.

In the past they have changed the laws and landscape of Britain and been at the forefront of numerous spiritual awakenings. They have flooded the church and cities with leaders, entrepreneurs and philanthropists, living for a different reward. They have taken seriously the commission to reach the world with the love of God and haven't been afraid to pay the price.

Whilst at university, they are learning to give beyond themselves, live beyond themselves and love their universities. At their best, they boldly engage in student culture with clean hearts and dirty hands. They see Christ in those they meet, the 'hope of glory'. They expose injustice and campaign to help others: other humans created in the image of God. They compassionately pray for the afflicted and the sick, expectant of an encounter with God's grace. They don't conform, but challenge the social, political and religious status quo. They transform and are transformed. They forcefully advance the kingdom and summon more of heaven here on earth.

My hope is that a move of God is stirring now in the student world and that students gripped by the love of God can and must help change the world.

Rod and Ruthie Gilbert

Rod and Ruthie Gilbert began ministry together with Scripture Union in India in the seventies, working initially in schools and camps. They then moved to Hebron School, India where Rod was Principal, and later returned to Scripture Union to start a family and marriage ministry, now known as Marriage Masala. They have four sons, one daughter and two grandsons and currently work in Sri Lanka.

Condensing our 'reasons for hope' into this short piece is a bit like trying to stuff a sleeping bag into a sock. But let's try, marking, as we call them, hope-stones down the last thirty years.

1977

One year after our marriage we stood next to a grave on a hillside in South India. The grave belonged to our first baby – a son – and we almost buried our hope for the future along with him. What gave us reason to hope again? We found these powerful verses in the Song of Solomon,

> Rise up, my love, my fair one, and come away. For lo, the winter is past . . . the time of singing has come. (2:10–12, NKJV)

When I was in hospital, one friend visited and silently hugged me for a long time. She then quietly left, but not before giving us a huge pile of Asterix comics. The paradox of deep grief and laughter brought us alive to hope again, and awoke a new depth of love for each other. This sustained us. Ten years later we stood in awe of our God of 'green hope' on that same hillside. That day we watched our four young children, laughing and chasing each other in the sunshine around the grassy grave. Hope fulfilled.

1987

One of our young Scripture Union Camp leaders shared our home after attempting suicide. Energetic and full of passion for life and his faith in Jesus, yet he had harboured bitter pain from the loss of his father as a teenager. How to renew his hope again? He discovered the joys in bathing babies, sorting out squabbling kids, and baking brownies. After the children were in bed we would agonizingly pray together. It was all he needed. Many years later we visited him in Australia, still living for God. There was a deep joy just in watching him and his young son playing in the local football team.

1997

We walked along a beach near Chennai, devastated and ready to pack our bags. Our eldest son had just told us he had been experimenting with drugs and had to leave school. Here we were, pioneering a vital new ministry with families, questioning if our own family was falling apart. As we kicked the sand in frustration, searching for an answer, God spoke to us in an almost audible voice, 'This is my ministry, not yours. I will build it!' We hung onto those words. The ministry was built through tough yet tremendously fulfilling years. A deep joy came eight years later when we held our eldest son's baby son in China – where he and his wife are passionately committed to laying down themselves for Jesus no matter what it takes. Hope being fulfilled!

Now, in Sri Lanka, where hope for this nation, torn by conflict and natural disaster, has all but faded in many people's minds, we continue to love and live for the God of hope: a hope that never fades.

David Muir

David Muir works with Christian Aid to engage churches and Christians in the issues of global poverty. He is passionate about bringing the gospel to the poor. David has also worked with local churches and Ichthus Christian Fellowship. He is married to Diane and has four sons.

I sat in my stuffy cabin in the bowels of a Greek cruise ship, looked at myself in the mirror and thought, 'So, now what?' It was late summer, 1977. I was the ship's DJ and had spent seven months gorging myself on all the pleasures that came with the job. A glut of travel and food, drink and drugs, sex and sun, music and cigars left me feeling jaded and sick in head, heart and stomach. I discovered how disillusioned you get when everything you ever wanted comes to you all at once.

Then the Jesus of book and history, as big as life, crossed the street and said to me, 'This way . . .' One year later I was a new man.

For much of my working life, the key challenge has been not to repeat the same kind of mistakes. No longer were sex and drugs the problem, but the pitfalls that came with my subsequent jobs. Working for churches, church networks and Christian organizations has been fascinating, and sometimes incredible. Christian jobs are, of course, not free from danger and temptation. To become disheartened with 'ministry' feels worse than becoming disillusioned with secular work.

But again, there was Jesus, on the other side of the street, crossing over and saying, 'This way . . .'

In recent years I've been working with the aid, relief and development agency, Christian Aid. The challenge now is not to be overwhelmed by world poverty, by the sheer size of the problems. In a world in which one billion are malnourished and one billion are overweight, a child dies every five seconds because she or he is hungry, a few hundred millionaires own as much wealth as the world's poorest two and a half billion people, and eight million die every year because they are simply too poor to keep themselves alive. It's not always easy to fend off disillusionment when faced with the harsh reality of our world.

Yet, Jesus still crosses the road and says, 'This way . . .' and one day he will make all things new.

Heather Wilson

Heather Wilson is a photographer and writer. A perpetual nomad, her passion to tell stories of the marginalized has led her around the globe; most recently she spent two and a half years in Afghanistan. Heather currently lives in Los Angeles.

> We are living in a world that is absolutely transparent and God is shining through it all the time. God manifests Himself everywhere, in everything, in people and in things and in nature and in events. The only thing is we don't see it.
>
> *Thomas Merton, Trappist monk and author*

So often I find the hope of God reflected through the faces and lives around me; one of the most remarkable being my friend, Haneefa. Though only seventeen years old, her capacity to bear life and draw it out of others is that of a grown, deep woman more than twice her age. From the moment I met her I was captivated by her laughter and won by the peace and joy she radiates.

Her father, valuing education, always sent his daughters to school along with the sons. Under the Taliban's regime this became impossible, so his wife secretly continued their education at home. Following the departure of the Taliban, both mother and father worked for a developmental NGO together, believing their country could be restored.

Two years ago Haneefa's mother died of cancer. Her father, since remarried, moved to an even more remote area, working with the NGO to promote education. This past year Haneefa joined her father in this, teaching in the girls' school along with teaching women's literacy courses.

In a couple of years the village has seen over two hundred young girls in three grades fill its building – the first time girls have been educated since the 1970s. Where literate women were scarce, there are now more than half a dozen classes of women learning to read and write. Haneefa's dream is to continue her education and to teach: she believes education is key to freedom, to peace and to understanding.

She and her father have won the trust of this conservative village, drastically altering the course of the future for its women and girls. Yet, when asked, Haneefa will tell you they've not done anything extraordinary. How many of our decisions have the potential to impact the lives of many?

Moving to Afghanistan in November of 2003, I went with a deep belief that God saw the country with hope, that there was more life yet to come for these people – who had experienced war for nearly as long as I had been alive. And I knew I wanted to be part of it. The years have weighed heavily, testing my faith beyond anything I could have imagined; having co-workers killed; watching the chasm between rich and poor only increase; knowing that one in six women still dies during childbirth; and that young girls continue to be married off long before the age of sixteen. I've discovered that holding hope doesn't mean that everything feels OK, nor does it rest upon the circumstances that surround me. Instead, it exists because God exists in this place.

On a good day, we hope that it doesn't rain or that we make our train on time, don't we? We hope that our football team wins the match or that we can shed those extra few pounds for summer. In Afghanistan I've found myself hoping that my friend will let his second wife finish her education, that another friend's husband will stop beating her, and that the anti-government elements will care more about the lives of Afghans than their suicide missions. The hardships take their toll on the country and on my own heart.

So, if God is present, if he has not forgotten the pain of the world, then what is his plan to meet this vast array of real needs? Where is his answer of hope to the young woman lying in a hospital bed, covered in burns after setting herself on fire when she could no longer handle living? Part of his answer is us! We are given the opportunity, every day, to either bring heaven to earth or to let hell remain. This is the choice God invites us to make when he says 'Love me – love people'. As we discover God more and more, as we discover his passion for us, we are compelled to engage with pain – because there is something great to be done for this world, a world that he deeply loves.

Despite the circumstances that can seem overwhelming in Afghanistan, I've found God's undeniable face of hope in the courage and love of the Afghans around me. My favourite Afghan proverb says, 'Drop by drop, a river is formed.' It is through daily choices that the love of God becomes a reality and that hope continues to grow in Afghanistan.

Ian Nicholson

Ian Nicholson has been involved in 24-7 Prayer, the global prayer and mission movement, since it started in 2000. He is currently on 24-7's international leadership team, helps lead the Guildford Boiler Room and is Director of the Matrix Trust, a local Christian charity. Ian lives with his family in Guildford.

Kneeling alone on a hard wooden floor in a classroom overlooking Guildford High Street was not the normal way I spent my Monday lunchtimes at school. 'Praying' to a Jesus I was not sure existed was also a first, but something very peculiar had been happening to me over those few days.

I suppose I was a pretty typical seventeen year old in 1973 (think cord flares, tank tops, Double Diamond beer, Embassy No. 6 cigarettes and T. Rex). I was into sport and girls and had a reputation as *the* Sixth Form drinker. I was not unhappy, lonely or bullied; I was just normal. I'd started feeling weird about God a few weeks before after an animated discussion at school. One night I shouted out loud, 'Anyway, God, even if you are there I want to have nothing to do with you!' The weird feelings left . . . for a while.

Then Grahame started sounding off in the pub one Saturday night and, a bit bored, I joined in. Considering he'd been a Christian all of two weeks he held his own pretty well against six of us. Those weird feelings came back and for all of the next day I bargained with 'God' that if a lamppost fell over or a person tripped up I would believe in him . . . nothing happened. Finally, on Monday I knelt on the floor and prayed a sincere, but quite agnostic prayer: 'Jesus, I don't even know if you exist but if you do, I need something in my life and I will follow you . . .'

This is where it gets difficult to communicate, but immediately I felt incredible peace; I felt I was floating, almost in another world. It felt different to anything I had felt before. It led to some dramatic changes and one friend said a few weeks later, 'If Ian Nicholson can give up getting drunk – there must be a God!'

To be honest . . . a weekend of weird feelings is not enough for a hope-filled life. Being a follower of Jesus for over thirty years has been much more about God's strength than mine: it's also been about the support of friends; understanding and trusting the Bible; asking some serious questions at times; and walking each day prayerfully with a God who is personal. However those weird feelings and a 'dodgy' prayer were 100 per cent real and a beginning: the start of the hope I base my life upon.

Pastor Bill Wilson

Bill Wilson, founder and senior pastor of Metro Ministries, Brooklyn, New York, has spent over twenty-five years in New York's inner city, where he and his staff have dedicated their lives to changing a generation . . . one child at a time. His ministry, including Kids Klub, has expanded all over the globe, reaching thousands of children in some of the toughest areas in the world.

To sit as a young boy for three whole days and three long nights on a street corner waiting for your mother to return and realizing that she isn't coming back for you – all you can do is hope. You hope any minute now she will walk around the corner and take you home. You hope very shortly she will come and pick you up, take you home where your stomach will be filled and you can lie down in warmth and safety. Twenty-four hours passes and still you wait. Forty-eight hours pass, hunger and loneliness set in. As the reality begins to dawn that she is not coming back, hopelessness becomes the only covering during the night silence. Day three dawns and still you wait. You hope someone will stop. At that point, all you have is hope. Then, as I have so often come to realize during my lifetime, it may come down to the last minute but if you hang in there, God comes. With no concept of God or Christian influence in my life, hope came during the third day in the form of a man called Dave Rudenis, who stopped to pick me up, even while his own son was dying of leukemia in the hospital. God came that day, didn't he?

Just a few days later, after Dave had paid my way to a Christian camp, I sat at an altar, having answered an invitation to give my life to Jesus. I hoped someone would pray with me. Every kid had a prayer counsellor with him or her, every kid except me. Yet that night God looked beyond the torn, smelly clothes and worn shoes and he saw my heart. That night 'hope' was birthed in my heart as I felt, for the first time in my life, that somebody loved me.

Who would ever have thought that one man picking up a poor boy left on the street would set in motion the largest Sunday school in the world reaching over forty thousand children weekly? Who would ever have conceived that one simple act would have global repercussions in the form of a ministry that is now circling the globe?

In all my experiences of life – the beatings, the stabbings, being shot, contracting hepatitis and tuberculosis while spending time in the garbage dumps and seeing twenty people murdered up close – the one factor that gives me hope to keep going, is that God uses ordinary people to do extra-ordinary things and through one person, can make a huge difference in many lives.

So, for the last forty years, I have been driving a Sunday school bus in New York every Saturday to pick up poor kids that need the message of hope through the gospel, then flying out somewhere different every weekend to preach and raise funds – funds to enable us to keep bringing hope to those who need to know that someone loves them. Who knows the potential in the kids we minister to each week and what they will go on to accomplish? The seemingly hopeless, receiving hope and going on to bring hope to the seemingly hopeless. For this man right here, and many more like me, it made all the difference, didn't it?

Your Hope

I trust that as you have read these testimonies they have inspired and encouraged you on your own personal journey.

Why don't you write down your own reason for hope? You could then pray about it and make sure it is inspiring all of your actions.

Through these testimonies it is clear that: true hope is only found in Jesus; this hope affects the way we live; people everywhere, in all different circumstances, are longing for a lasting hope; and we need to share our hope with others.

We all live real lives in a real world. Problems to do with money or relationships, health or careers don't just disappear. However, the stories show us that anyone can call on God and can cast all their cares onto him. His wisdom and support transform our lives.

If you are already a Christian you too have a story to tell. Don't just keep hope to yourself. Your hope needs to be communicated to your neighbours, your colleagues, even the person that you sit next to on the train or in the coffee shop. Let your hope shine in your life and be prepared to take a risk and tell others.

If you're not a Christian, can I suggest you find out more about this life of hope?

Hope is available to you whatever your condition or circumstances. It's available to the addict who feels unable to break free. Hope is available to the teenage girl who's broken up with her boyfriend. Hope is available to the rich businessman who still feels lonely deep down. It's available to those who have lost someone and it's available to all those who just want to know what life's all about.

True hope is available *now* to everyone, and it can only be found in Jesus Christ who died and rose again. Why not put your hope in him today?